I0122736

Living Fire
&
God's Law of Life

**Sacred Wisdom & Knowledge
of the Ancients**

Professor Hilton Hotema

ISBN: 978-1-63923-118-8

Printed: January 2022

Cover Art By: Paul Amid

Published and Distributed By:
Lushena Books
607 Country Club Drive, Unit E
Bensenville, IL 60106
www.lushenabks.com

ISBN: 978-1-63923-118-8

Table of Contents

Prologue

Happy indeed am I to have this rare pleasure and opportunity of writing this Prologue for my highly esteemed friend, Professor Hilton Hotema, whom I've known for many years. He was born in 1878 and still feels like forty, being a living example to prove the value of his remarkable teachings in the matter of health and longevity. And I, born in 1883, also feel like forty due to my good fortune of finding the teachings of Professor Hilton many years ago and following them as closely as possible in this world of artificialism erroneously called civilization.

Professor Hotema says for us to go to the Bugs and Birds and learn the Lesson of Life; for they have no illness, no doctors, no hospitals, no vaccines, no serums, no poisons erroneously called medicine, and yet they are ruled by the same law that governs man.

Look not to the schools to learn the facts of Life. They are not established for that purpose. They are controlled by standardized systems which stagnate progress, and their work is to brainwash the man and condition the mind so as to control the Masses.

Fichte laid it down that "education" should aim at destroying free will so that, after pupils have left school, they shall be incapable, thruout the rest of their lives, of thinking or acting otherwise than as their schoolmasters would have wished (*Age of Treason* by R. S. Clymer).

The Mother Church declares it is a crime to permit Freedom of Thought, as it leads man into error. Man should be taught by the Church what to think and not be allowed to think otherwise.

The book called the Bible did not exist until the 5th century of our era. The work of making it was begun in 325 A.D. by Eusebius of Caesarea, and he died before it was completed. Then the work was taken over by a young fanatic named Jerome and completed by him in the 5th century. That first Bible was called the Vulgate because its language was so common.

The Bible is a book of fables and fiction, of symbols and allegories; and the great Kabalist Eliphas Levi said, "No one can understand a single sentence in the Bible without the Key to the Sacred Numbers." And the Protestant Preachers have not that Key. If they did have it, they would know that the last book of the Bible teaches the ancient secret of Regeneration in one of the most stupendous allegories ever penned by the hand of man.

The secret of Regeneration is presented in the form of a drama, expressed in terms of natural phenomena. Its hero is the Sun, its heroine the Moon; and all the other characters are Planets, Stars, and Constellations, while its stage-setting comprises the Sky, the Earth, the Rivers, and the Sea. It elucidates its subject with the glare of the lightning, proclaims it with the roll of thunder, emphasizes it with the shock of the earthquake, and reiterates it with the Ocean's voice, the ceaseless murmur of its "many waters."

Ever it maintains this cosmic phraseology, this vast phrasing of Nature. And then, from his effulgent throne, the Solar Entity announces, "Behold" I am making a new Universe." Now this Apocalyptic Universe is Man, the lesser cosmos, of whom the Sun is in fact the Architect and Builder and whom the Moon and all the Stars of heaven have helped to mold and make.

For in every human being, however fallen and degraded, are stored up all the forces, both cosmic and deific, which brought him into existence and have nurtured him thru out the vast cycle of generations, in countless incarnations upon the earth. And these same creative forces, with the tireless patience of the deathless Gods, but await the time when the resurgent Divine Life again stirs within him; and then this child of the aeons, whom the Demon of Darkness can drag down till he is lower than the beasts, the Eagle of Light can exalt above the clouds.

San Diego, California
Dr. M. F. Schrader
September 27, 1959.
By Bunnie Boyden, Secretary

Chapter 1
Interlaced Triangles

The scraps of ancient scriptures that have come down to us show that in the Golden Age of Man, when Astrological Science and Ancient Philosophy walked hand-in-hand in perfect harmony, the fundamental principles of Creation were formulated by the Ancient Masters and presented in the Ageless Wisdom, preserved in the Bible in symbology and allegory and in other ancient literature.

The geometrical symbol of Number Six is the Interlaced Triangles forming the Six-Pointed Star, called by the Hindus the Sign of Vishnu and by the Hebrews the Shield of David and the Seal of Solomon. With the Egyptians it was the Symbol of Creation, the unition of Fire and Water, the Male and Female elements.

The Interlaced Triangles signified the triune God reflected in His Creations. "The trinity of nature is the lock," wrote Eliphas Levi, "and the trinity of Man is the Key that fits it." It also signified the Six Creative Groups, the Six Powers in Nature, the Six Planes of Consciousness and of Evolution, and the Six Principles of Man, all of which are synthesized in the Seventh.

In the ancient Kabalah, the First Trinity of Creation is called the Macroprosopus and the second the Microprosopus, the two constituting the Greater and Lesser Countenances. The former is the Living Fire and the letter the Reflected Fire. the Supreme Triangle and its Reflection, forming the Six-Pointed Star when interlaced. The White Triangle, pointing upward, symbolized Siva, Fire, Light, Celestial Powers and also the Divine Trinity in Man, ever evolving upward after its incarnation in matter, seeking more expression on a higher level.

The Black Triangle, pointing downward, symbolized the Dark Waters of Chaos, in which the Divine Germ is laid and also the instability of man's lower nature, "as unstable as water."

The Black Triangle also indicated that the two descending lines of force can ascend from their focus (apex) on the earth and reach up to and unite with the Divine. The symbolism of the Interlaced Triangles reveals the secret of the biblical statement that the Created resembles the Creator; that image and like-of the Creator (Genesis 1:26, 27). And so, the Masters said, "As above, so below." The reality back of this symbol is that as the Creative Attributes are not only reflected in man, but interlaced and balanced in him, the Microcosm, the Mighty Magician, and all forces within him and Nature are dominated by him.

Thus, Number Six is the symbol of the ever-changing, ever-becoming cosmic phenomena, rising from the stream of Creative Essence which manifests in all things, on all planes, as the Animative Principle called Life. The Solar Orb is the focusing point; for as the Sun pours out its life-giving, fructifying power — sheds its symbolical blood — can the Living Fire manifest the various forms on the earth and evolve them to perfection.

The great secret of Life we learn in Number Six. It expresses the Astral Realm and reveals the Knowledge of Good and Evil. In the Intellectual World it indicates the balance between liberty and necessity; and in the Physical World, the antagonism of natural forcing, the linking of Cause and Effect, of Form and Essence.

Number Six signifies two actions, or twice three. It does not represent forces in equilibrium, but a constant oscillation between action and reaction. It thus indicates a wavering, a vacillation, or forces so uncontrolled and ill-directed that they tend to destroy one another.

Number Six shows that the cause of all evolution is the urge toward perfection, inherent in all living things. The urge results in the conscious adaptation of the living organism to its environment, in contradistinction to the stupid scientific theory that evolution results from a blind, mechanical reaction of the organism to a hostile environment.

The inherent urge toward Perfection is the practically unknown power which sustains the body in health when not obstructed and which restores the sick body to health when not prevented by the work of a stupid doctor with his poisonous remedies and dangerous methods.

The urge toward Perfection is symbolized by the geometrical formation of the figure Six itself. In the verticle line is the One Life, the Living Fire, descending from the astral realm and manifesting within the O of the Microcosm in the physical realm.

The O of the 6 may also be considered as the Microcosm which contains all of man's latent powers, while the line extending upward symbolizes the unrest and aspiration of the Ego, which is determinedly reaching upward and endeavoring always to manifest ever greater degrees of Divinity. Occult science says this is also Jacob's Ladder, the Antaskarana, along which the Angels (Living Fire) are continually descending and ascending (Genesis 28:12).

Occultists hold that the Sixth Principle in man is Buddhi, or the Divine Principle, which cannot rest at ease until it attains its Perfect Manifestation in Number Seven, the subject-matter of Revelation, last book of the Bible.

"This composite nature of man," wrote Dr. Arthur A. Beale, "involves the concept of Seven Grades of Consciousness; the three higher (triad) all separately self-conscious, each one in sequence communicating with the illuminating that inferior to it; and a quaternary of four grades of substance, intermixed, each with its own vibratory rate and so permitting various grades of consciousness to function thru them. This quaternary represents man as we know him and is dominated by a stream of consciousness flowing from the Higher (Luminous) Triad" (*Evolution of Mind*. p. 20)

The urge toward Perfection causes the six-sided cube of purely animal ran to evolve into the Cross, the verticle stem composed of four parts and the horizontal of three. And so, upon this Cross of Matter the Astral Man is crucified on the terrestrial plane until the lower square of the vertical portion has been raised up and drawn into the one next above, thus forming the Solar Cross, the Cross of Life, with four equal arms.

Man cannot be at ease until he has found the Light, knows the secret of his Solar Being, recognizes that he is one with the Creator, the Reflected Image of the Absolute, and that the same Creative Force works in him as in all Nature, to bring forth Perfection.

In the first chapter of Genesis appears the order of the Seven Ages and Seven Stages of the earth's evolution, and their symbolism is presented by that great Kabalist, Eliphas Levi, in his "*Unpublished Letters,*" as follows:

1st day of Creation: The light splendid and radiant, Unity.

2nd day: The firmament, or the necessary separation between Spirit and Matter, between the celestial and terrestrial realms.

3rd day: Germination of the earth under the influence of solar radiation. Germination begins with the revelation of the ternary.

4th day: The Sun and Moon rule over day and night. Division of all the seasons by the quaternary. Primiti ve quadrature of the circle.

5th day: Life appears in the bosom of the elements; constitution of the kingdom of man is the Number Five.

6th day: The earth and fire respond to air and water and produce the living realm; the triangle, which is the reflection of that J. H. V. H., forms itself in the body of man; and the Inner Voice says to him, "Facimus Hominem," for a man must share in his own creation.

7th day: On the Seventh Day, the Creator rested; that is, the Septenary being the Perfect Number, there remains nothing more to be done.

Levi added: "No one can understand a single sentence in the Bible without the Key to the Sacred Numbers." The Blazing Triangle is the reflection of J.H.V.H., and the biblical makers cleverly deceived the profane and exoteric by arbitrarily vowel zing these initial letters to produce the word Je-Ho-Vah, giving a new name to the "God (who) spake unto Moses," but making no explanation for the reason of so doing (Exodus 6:3). One of the golden secrets of the Ancient Masters is cleverly concealed in these four initial letters J.H.V.H. They have such a vital relation to the Creative Process that the time has come when the secret should be revealed, and Hotema has revealed it in the *Flame Divine*.

And as this is done, the exoteric and profane, the Catholic and Protestant, the priest and the preacher, will be amazed when shown the directly connecting link existing between J.H.V.H. and Sphinx, the Four Beasts of Ezekiel and Daniel, and the Four Beasts before the throne in Revelation (Ezekiel 1:1-34; Daniel 7:1-7; Revelation 4:6,7). The Sixth Commandment says: "Thou shalt not kill" (Exodus 20:130). The only sense in which man can kill is to damage or injure the living organism so seriously that the Cosmic Stream of Living Fire will no longer flow thru it.

The Bible says the conquest of Death is the last victory; that Death shall be swallowed up in victory; "and there shall be no more death." "O death, where is thy sting? O grave, where is thyvictory." — Isaiah 25:8; 1 Corinthians 15:55; Revelation 21:4).

That last, final, and sublime victory is not and will not be gained by any change that will ever occur in the fixed and immutable laws of Creation. That victory is and will be gained by greater knowledge as to the facts of Life. For the facts of Life, when better known and understood, will change the mental state of man; and when that change has occurred, "the former things (which man believed) are passed away" (Revelation 21:4).

The Ageless Wisdom of the Ancient Masters teaches us that the Divine Trinity is reflected in man; and this knowledge, when correctly and clearly interpreted as Hotema has presented it in his various works, will lift the veil that darkens the Mind and reveal to the understanding of man the facts of Eternal Life.

Chapter 2
Lights

Knowledge based upon the actual facts of Creation enlighten the Mind, and the teachings of that nature are opposed by the Standardized Systems of the institutions that rule civilization.

In allegory the Bible says, "He carried me away in the Spirit (trance) to a great and high mountain (Man's head) and showed me the Great City (Man) the Holy Jerusalem, descending out of heaven" (Revelation 21:10). In all creation there is nothing higher than the human head. Man's feet rest upon the earth; but his head, symbolically speaking, reaches up into the clouds.

Nor is there anything in the world that is holier than Man. "For within him is the Kingdom of God, making him the Temple of God; and in God he lives and moves and has his being" (Luke 17:21; Acts 17:28; Corinthians 3:16). Therefore, look not for anything holier than Man.

Man is the Microcosm of the Macrocosm. He is a miniature Universe containing within himself in some form or other, according to the Bible, everything contained in the Universe, whether it be forces or substance. Hence, Man is in fact, as well as in fable, an organized Universe, the Holy Jerusalem that descended from the Celestial World, his eternal home.

In the great Universe there are countless revolving planets, suns, and stars. So, in man there are numberless atoms, revolving round a center, as far apart from one another as the stars are from one another relatively speaking. A single cell of man's body is a miniature Universe in itself. For everything in the great Universe has its correspondence in man's body, active or passive, known or unknown. And the City (man's body) had no need of the Sun, neither of the Moon, to shine in it; for the Glory of God did lighten it. ... And the gates of it (orifices of the body) shall not be shut at all by day; for there shall be no night there (in the body) (Revelation 21:23, 25).

And the City lieth four-square, and the length is as large as the breadth, the Cube of Space, composed of the Sacred Four Elements, symbolized by the Sphinx, described in all the great religious systems of antiquity and designated in the Bible as the Four Beasts round about the throne which represent the physical, fluidal, aerial, and astral Man (Revelation 4:6,7; 21:16).

After the Foundation Stone was laid Four Square, Man followed and is symbolized in the Arcane Science by number Five, the most deeply occult of all the digits; and few there be who can grasp full significance of what it represents in their evolution and accomplishment.

In the Ageless Wisdom, Five symbolized Man in a dual aspect. He inhabits two worlds. In his animal nature he is a member of the Animal Kingdom; but in his Spiritual Nature he rises to the summit of all Creation and dwells in the Celestial World of Angelism.

The terrestrial and celestial worlds meet and blend in Man, as represented by the Interlaced Triangles, described elsewhere. And furthermore, "Man is the universally structured type," said Edward Whipple, who added: "In one aspect all the lower types rise toward man and are completed in him." Man not only contains within himself all the principles and elements that appear in manifested nature, but during his intrauterine development, he passes thru stages analogous to the various kingdoms, the vegetable, fish, reptile, animal, and up to the humanal, finally rising to the angelical. Hence, Man is truly a synthesis of the Macrocosm. "As above, so below."

It was this discovery in the 19th century which constrained Darwin and others to believe they had solved the secret of man. And to this good day the text-books of the schools and colleges are filled with this erroneous conception and conclusion — that Man is an improved ape.

Number Five is composed of 4 and 1, or the Sacred Four and the Spiritual Man, manifesting on the physical plane, thus determining Man's real constitution, not yet discovered by science and so admitted by the great Dr. Alexis Carrel, who wrote:

"Our knowledge of the human body is, in fact, most rudimentary. It is impossible, for the present, to grasp its constitution" (*Man The Unknown*, p. 119).

The Pentalpha of Pythagoras was the Five-Pointed Star, resembling Five Alphas, joined at their bases. The Mystic Wand, said to have been used by Moses and Aaron and all Initiates, is described as a Rod with a Five-Pointed Star at its end, with which it is said are performed all magical rites.

Before this Magic Symbol every elemental force must bow. According to that great Kabalist Eliphas Levi: "The Empire of the Will over the Astral Light, which is the physical Soul of the Four Elements, is represented in magic by the Pentagram. Man himself is this Pentagram. With his head erect, his hands outstretched, and his feat spread apart, he forms the Living Five Pointed Star.

Standing upon the Cube of Creation formed by the Sacred Four, with hands upraised in praise of the Almighty, and brain active to interpret the reports of his Five Senses, he dominates all the Kingdoms. But he must first dominate himself; and there is where he fails, as the history of humanity testifies, according to the interpretation of the Black Pentacle, which appears in another place. The Radiating Light, said to flow from the Five Points of the Pentacle at the end of the Magic Wand, symbolizes the powers inherent in the perfected body of Man. For when Man's Five Senses are illuminated by the Living Fire, they radiate the

Spiritual Powers by which he can perform all the miracles of Life, as taught in the Ancient Mysteries.

The secret significance of this Symbol, the Blazing Star of Bethlehem (Matthew 2:2), is that as Man expands his Consciousness by higher development, by regeneration, he becomes indeed a Magician, as the clairvoyant or the hypnotist, and is capable of performing the White or Black Magic of the Masters. It was taught by the Masters that this is accomplished by raising up from the Creative Centers at the base of the spinal column the Living Fire of Creation that is symbolized in various ways in the Bible, but especially by the Fiery Serpent of Moses (Numbers 21:8, 9), and the Conqueror on the White Horse, whose "eyes were as a flame of fire," indicating the illumination of man's Five Senses on all planes of being (Revelation 19:11, 12).

The Flaming Pentacle also symbolized Man's erect head and up-lifted hand, with invisible fire flowing from his Five Fingers, symbolized in the Bible by the parable of the Five Wise Virgins who kept their lamps trimmed and burning, the inverted Pentacle, symbolized by the Black Five-Pointed Star, signifying the Five Foolish Virgins with dark lamps who could not enter (Matthew 25; 1-12). Among the Greeks the Pentacle was held so sacred that on the lintels of their Temples where the numerals were carved, number Five was inlaid with pure gold. This numeral was also carved on an amulet and worn around the neck by the Greeks and Romans as protection against evils. The Sacred Words of Brahma, "Zama, Zama Ozza Rachama Ozai," when translated, read, "The Robe, the Glorious Robe of my strength."

This meant that Five represents the Five Mystic Powers which must be attained and man infested thru the Robe of Flesh (body) by the Resurrected Initiate, after being symbolically slain and spending Three Days in the Tomb, ere he can attain the

Great Initiation, indicated in the Bible by the "Resurrection of Jesus," and in Masonry by the symbolical "slaying and resurrection" of the candidate, (as stated by Edmond Ronaye in his book, *"Freemasonry,"* P. 219).

These Five High Powers rise from the enfoldment, development, and employment of Man's Five Senses on the Inner Plane of Consciousness, the Kingdom of God within, unrecognized by modern man, but discovered by the Masters, whom science terms "superstitious heathens," and preserved in the Bible, which science regards as a book of fairy tales for children.

We shall show in our consideration of the Black Pentacle that Man's Five Senses are dimmed as with a veil, due to consumption of the Living Fire on the animalistic plane of propagation and to "mind conditioning" that results from the brainwashing process of the schools. It is only in rare cases that there appears a person who is capable of extending the function of his senses to the Divine Kingdom within. This subject is so large and important that we lack space here to give it more consideration. But when Man dons "The Robe of his Strength," he finds the functioning of his senses surprisingly extended as far beyond the physical as the range of a color is extended by the multiplication of its shadings.

And, more surprising, out of the synthesis of these extended senses, there evolves the latent Sixth Sense, called Premonition, which is incomprehensible to him who is confined to a more limited use of his senses. And from the activation of the Sixty, there also rises the function of the latent Seventh, called Clairvoyance, symbolized in the Bible in various ways; in the Gospels as 5 loaves and 2 fishes (Matthew 14:17), and in Revelation, in one instance, as the "marriage of the Lamb" (Revelation 19:7). This was one of the golden secrets of the Masters; and it was the strange experiences of these higher levels of Consciousness to which Paul alluded when he said they were "unlawful to utter," or to reveal to the Profane. This is mentioned as "the Seven Thunders" in Revelation, and the message was "sealed up" and not recorded in the Bible, nor exposed to the Profane (Revelation 10: 3, 4).

The body, thus glorified by the Five Supernal Powers, was called the Robe of Initiation. The Great Initiation had not been accomplished until the Neophyte had donned this Robe and manifested in the flesh his higher powers of Consciousness.

The Blazing Star reminds Man that he is Animal, Humanal, and Angelical, dwelling in the Lower Kingdom to bless or to curse in proportion to the degree in which he makes a true balance and metes out just weight in accordance with the law; and he rises to the Higher Kingdom as he subdues his animalistic nature, allegorized in the Bible as "killing the beast" (Proverbs 9:2), thus conserving the Living Fire at the base of the spine so it will ascend to the brain and activate the latent organs of Premonition and Clairvoyance, the Pituitary and Pineal glands respectively. That is the "marriage of the Lamb." And so, at the entrance to the Path of Attainment appeared the first injunction, "Man, know Thyself and thou wilt know the Universe," and the second, "Eat not of the Forbidden Fruit" (Genesis 2:17).

For only as Man knows his Divine Power; has recognized his physical pairs of opposites, has diligently collected all he finds in his lower self and cast it into the crucible for purification, and conserved his Vital Essence of Life, can he truly know himself. For he stands in the center of his Universe and is responsible, under the Law of Cause and Effect, for the use of the powers which exalt him to the heights of Angelical Attainment, or sink him lower than the beasts.

Our Magic Wand with its Blazing Star must first be turned inward to the *Kingdom of Heaven,* and we must fully and truly realize that the Human Body is the greatest Temple ever created and is the Sacred Temple in which abides The Spirit of God.

The Ancient Masters believed what they taught, and their Temples of Worship were patterned after the Human Temple in which the Spiritual Man dwells, a fact proven by a study of the ground-plan of either the Sanctuary at Karnack or of the Temple of Solomon, in which a design of the Seven Principle Nerve Centers of the body was inlaid upon the ceiling in the form of Seven Golden Disks, each distinguished by the seven colors or the solar spectrum. No one can appreciate the marvelous teachings of the Bible until one is able to interpret the allegories and understand the inner meaning of such statements as "Wisdom hath builded her house (Human Body); "she hath hewn out her Seven Pillars" (Seven Sense Powers) (Proverbs 9:1).

The acquisition of the Golden Key of Humanal Salvation thru self-knowledge was the Great Goal toward which the masters of all ages have labored. But in this boastful modern age, the direction of the Quest has changed; and the principle objective now is to keep Man in Darkness so as to make his enslavement the more sure and certain.

The various organizations and institutions which control civilization and pretend to teach useful knowledge for human betterment do nothing more than brainwash the man and condition his Mind to accent more freely the Standardized Systems by which he is so securely bound.

In his great book, *The Age of Treason* (1957), Dr. R.S. Clymer said:

"Fear those who, by usurped power, have the means to destroy man's reason and manhood, thereby making him an unreasoning being, a robot, or zombie, and preventing him from fulfilling his Divine Destiny by making his Soul's awakening impossible."

Chapter 2
Darkness

And men loved darkness rather than light because their deeds were evil. For everyone that doeth evil hateth the light, neither cometh the light, lest their deeds should be reproved (John 3:19, 20).

How perfectly that statement fits in the days of this generation which doeth evil as great as any of those which preceded it, back, back, back, into the dark night of time.

We have shown that Five is the number of Humanity in the Ageless Wisdom and symbolized man in a dual aspect. A Blazing Pentacle, the Eastern Star of Freemasonry, represents Man standing upright, feet resting on the earth and head reaching up high into the clouds, while the Black Pentacle of the Ancient Mysteries represented Man focusing his Five Senses downward on the lower planes of life. In the Black Pentacle, Man's head rests on the earth, his arms are bound behind him, and his feet extend up into the air, presented in Card No. 12 of the ancient Tarot as the Hanged Man, feet up and head down.

All the various commentators on the twenty-two Trumps Major of the Tarot appeared lost in the wilderness when they met the man hanging by his feet. Not one we encountered saw that this strange symbol signifies the Darkened Mind of him who lives by sight in the world of illusion, which seems to stable, but is changing constantly, like a flowing stream in which the water of yesterday is not the water of today. And furthermore, the Hanged Man with head down signifies man as using his head to invent dark schemes and his hands to desecrate that which is good, while grasping for worldly things at the expense of his fellowman.

His feet up in the air implies that he is trampling the Creator, and turning his powers downward to pervert his days and poison his life. He is immersed in materialism and aspiring toward self-aggrandizement instead of serving humanity. All the sin, sickness, suffering, persecution, hatred, and antagonism manifesting in the world are the result of Man's reversal or perversion of the Sacred Pentacle, i.e., himself and his powers.

The Demon of Humanity is the Darkness created by established institutions and organizations which control civilization with standardized systems, the worst of which in this age is perhaps medical art. The Man of Darkness is looking for Light when he seeks membership in the Masonic Lodge, where the word Light conveys a far more recondite meaning than that possessed by the masses. It is the first of all Symbols explained to the candidate and continues to be presented to him in various forms thru out all his future progress in his Masonic career.

Freemasons are emphatically called the Sons of Light because they are, or at least are entitled to be, in possession of the real meaning of the Symbol, while the profane or uninitiated are, by a parity of expression, said to be in Darkness. But these Sons of Light know not that their teachers and leaders possess very little more Light as to the Mysteries of Life and Creation than do the profane and exoteric. The connection of material Light with this emblematic and mental illumination was prominently presented in all the ancient religions and in the esoteric Mysteries.

In the latter only were the profound mysteries of Life and Creation fully explained to the candidate by the Masters who produced the Ageless Wisdom.

Among the Egyptians, the hare was the hieroglyphic of eyes that are open, as that little animal was believed to have its eyes always open. The Masters later adopted the hare as the Symbol of Moral Illumination revealed to the candidate in the contemplation of the Divine Truth and, hence, it was also a symbol of the Egyptian Osiris (Light), according to Champollion. Since Light was adored as the source of God, Darkness was abhorred as the source of Evil; causing the rise of the doctrine which prevailed among the ancients that two antagonistic principles were continually contending for the ruling of the world.

These two opposing conditions in which man lived, occasioned by the pleasure of Light and the repugnance of Darkness, induced him to imagine the existence of two antagonistic forces in Nature, to whose dominion he was alternately subjected; and they were symbolized in the Egyptian Mythology as Osiris, who represented Light, and Typhon, who represented Darkness.

In the Ancient Mysteries, this reverence for Light as an emblematic representation of the Principle of Good was predominant. And so, the candidate passed thru scenes of utter darkness during his initiation and at length terminated his trails by admission to the splendidly illuminated sacellum, where he was said to have attained Pure and Perfect Light Mentally and where he received the necessary instructions which were to invest him with knowledge of the mysteries of Life and Creation, which were the object of all his labors.

Initiation in the Ancient Mysteries meant much more to the seeker of Light than it ever has in any lodge, order, or system since the Mysteries were crushed in the 4th, 5th, and 6th centuries of our era. They were crushed for one reason because they taught the mysteries of Life and Creation in understandable forms and in scientific terms for it is difficult to enslave Man by fear of the future beyond the grave when he intelligently understands the secret of Life.

That is another reason why the world today is so destitute of scientific knowledge as to the secret of Life. One of the greatest scientists of modern times declared publicly that he could not explain why he was alive rather than dead; and another great scientist exclaimed:

'In fact, our ignorance (of life) is profound. ... Man is composed of a procession of phantoms, in the midst of which there strides an Unknowable Reality....Our knowledge of the body is, in fact, most rudimentary. It is impossible, for the moment, to grasp its constitution...Men of science know not where they are going' (Dr. Alexis Carrel, in (*Man The Unknown*)

Such dense ignorance does not just happen. It is the result of a deep plot. It is so intended by the schools and colleges and by the Standardized Systems which control this civilization.

Leading scientists, such as Dr. George W. Crile, Professor George Lakhovsky and others, have discovered and disclosed the nature of Life, but their works are ignored because the knowledge is not wanted. It would explode the postulates of the Holy Hierarchies of Science, upset Christianity, and ruin medical art. That is why men are kept in darkness and taught to like it.

Man is born in a world that is new and strange to him. And the Standardized Systems which rule civilization are so organized as to prevent him from finding the Light. They are designed to keep him in Darkness. Man comes into a world where he is surrounded by mysteries. His life and his senses are mysteries to him, and he is a mystery to himself. All he can ever learn must be acquired by him via his senses, and they usually deceive him and lead him astray; for he seldom sees what he thinks he sees.

What do we know of Substance? Science even doubts that it exists. qualities, but not the thing itself. Scientists assert that if the vortexial action of all solid matter in or on the earth were arrested, the resultant mass would form a ball no bigger than an average pumpkin.

And what a mystery are the action of cold and heat upon the wondrous fluid called water. It forms from invisible vapor, and more cold changes it to ice, so strong it will sustain elephants — presenting the phenomenon of gigantic animals standing on invisible vapor. Unbelievable but true.

What is Substance? Does it fill all space and exist as invisible vapor? And can it be transformed into everything known? Are we material Entities constituted of nothing but invisible rays? Do we dissolve as ice and float off in space as ice does? Does cosmic law ever change? Does it have exceptions or fail to apply to everything known and unknown? No philosopher believes that. Nor can science furnish logical answers for most of these questions.

These are mysteries that defy human intelligence. They reveal how little we can ever know about the mysteries of the Universe° And equally absurd is the claim of medical art that it can conquer "disease."

Man's work can never nullify the great law of Cause and Effect. We shall always reap just as we sow, medical art and the Mother Church to the contrary. "God so loved the world that he gave his only begotten Son, that whosoever believeth in him should not perish, but have everlasting life" is a nice tale for children and an interesting fable for adults in darkness, but it cannot deceive the Son Of Light (John 3:16).

Learn the Law of Life and obey it and human ailments will vanish. Proof of this appears everywhere in those who are never ill. They are not just lucky nor immune to the effects of transgression. They live more in harmony with the law, as do the bugs and birds; and their logical reward is health.

This is all too simple and understandable for the masses in Darkness. Complexity and confusion are the thrillers. They attract the foolish multitude. Anything that can be understood is worthless. Only the wise are impressed and inspired by Creation's Great Simplicity.

Consider what would happen if some phase of cosmic law were suddenly suspended, that of attraction, or affinity, or cohesion, for instance. The whole material world, with its rocks and trees, its beds of coal, our own bodies, and the very elements of this apparently indestructible earth, would instantaneously dissolve into invisible vapor of infinitely minute particles of atoms, diffused thru infinite space. Think if puny Man, with his limited senses, endeavoring to grasp and comprehend the mysteries of Life and Creation. Infinite space, stretching out from him in all directions, without limit. Infinite time, without beginning or ending. And Man in the center of each, like a helpless pebble upon the shore of the sea.

Bound up within our frail frame is the mighty Entity we call Ego for lack of a better term. And that eternal Entity spurns the narrow span of all visible existence, ever reaching outward thus striving for freedom from its prison. It gazes forth from the grated windows of our senses upon the limitless reaches of endless space, knowing that beyond the walls in which it is confined there lies the infinite paths to Eternal Freedom.

Everything within and without us should move our minds to admiration and our intellect to amazement. Man is a mystery encompassed with mystery. The connection of Mind with Matter, of Life with Physical Form, are a mystery. And equally mysterious are the marvelous communication lines, extending from the brain to every part of the body and from the brain reaching upward thru the Fontioulus Frontalis in the crown of the head, mentioned in the Bible as a door in heaven (Revelation 4; 1) into the vast Auriferous Realm surrounding the earth and containing everything appearing in the visible world as cosmic phenomena, usually called Nature.

Consider the mysterious link called tin Silver Cord in the Bible (Ecclesiasts 12:6), not yet discovered by science, which unites the Kingdom of Heaven within to the Kingdom of Heaven without, mentioned in the Bible as Jacob's Ladder (Genesis 28:12) and revealing the secret of the statement that in God we live and move and have our being (Acts 17: 28).

This is a scientific statement, covering the solid fact of existences, and not light poetry for children nor a figment of the imagination of "superstitious heathens."

The Created are united with the Creator by a radar beam as certain as the rising of the sun and as mysterious as a ray of solar light that causes the flowers of the field to bend their forms to the east at dawn and to the west at dusk. For who is so ignorant and vain as to believe that he is free and independent of the sustaining power of Creation? No one but modern scientists, evolutionists, and their stupid followers.

The power of movement is as much of a mystery as the power of thought. And inexplicable are memory and dreams, which reach beyond the limits of space and time and are the echoes of past and previous incarnations, as taught by the Ancient Masters. For the major mysteries of Life are logically and satisfactorily solved only by the Law of Reincarnation,

The fact of Reincarnation, so far from being mysterious and difficult of proof, is really very prosaic and simple so that it was always treated as exoteric in all archaic religions and philosophies. Positive evidence of its truth, on the basis of personal experience, was one of the first lessons learned by him who was initiated in the Ancient Mysteries. The same ritual in Freemasonry is but an empty mockery of the original which it copied from the Mysteries of the Ancient Masters.

Light flows from knowledge based on the facts of life, and Darkness rises like a fog from ignorance. That which we don't understand is mysterious. The schools, colleges, and educational systems are the source of the ignorance that creates mysteries. They are more concerned with the scheme of Mental Darkness and Mind Control than with the desire to spread the Light of Knowledge.

But the schools would be glad to teach the facts of Life if they were not denied that great privilege by the Powers That Be, which rule civilization by Standardized Systems that stagnate all progress.

They produce a whirlpool in which all things move in a circle; and while that may be termed "progress," it is a kind of progress that never takes us any nearer to the core, in which are concealed the mysteries of Life and Creation. And to sustain these Systems of Stagnation, the ruling Hierarchies reject all facts and evidence which fail to agree with their established dogmas. Even in the ancient world, the sordid Priesthood, with its natural proclivities, employed its powers not to improve the condition of humanity nor to enlighten the masses, but to build wider and stronger the fabric of its own world, which rested upon the bowed backs of the deceived masses. The amazing discoveries of the Ancient Masters were concealed from all but those found worthy to receive the precious knowledge. But the purity of their purpose deteriorated in time, and their corruption produced their own destruction.

Rank and dignity succeeded to the original simplicity. Unprincipled, vain, insolent, corrupt, venal men put on the Creator's livery, not to serve humanity, but to further their own evil designs. Luxury, greed, vice, intolerance, and pride deposed frugality, virtue, kindness, and humility, changing the altar where servants should instruct, to a throne on which despots reigned and ruled.

Chapter 4
Magic Wand

Among the Symbols of the Ancient Masters appeared two regarded as Magic Wands. One is described as a Rod with a Pentacle at its end, with which it was said all magical rites were performed, as we have explained under Light. The other was the Caduceus, the symbolism of which so little known, that medical art, in its stupidity, uses it as its emblem, yet it has no relation at all to "medicine': and perhaps no doctor is competent to interpret its symbolism.

Encyclopedias should, but do not for good reasons, contain a long account of the Caduceus. For it was one of the most important of all the ancient Symbols. It was borne by Hermes or Mercury and by Cybele, Minerva, Anubis, Hercules, Ogminus the God of the Celts, and the personified Constellation of Virgo.

In Freemasonry the Staff of the Senior Deacon, or Master of Ceremonies, is an analogue of the Caduceus, but he who would be able to interpret its esoteric meaning would be a big exception to the rule.

The essence of this Symbol extends back to the Edenic Parable in Genesis and to the last book of the Bible. It relates to the Tree of Life, to the Creative Principle of the Universe, to the Creative Power of Man, to the Burning Bush of Moses (Exadus 3:1-4)A to the Fiery Serpent upon a pole (Numbers 21:8), to the candlestick, with bowl on top of it, with two olive trees on the sides, and the Two Anointed Ones that stand by the Lord of the whole earth (Zechariah 4:2, 3, 11-14), to the Book with Seven Seals, the Beast with seven Heads, and the Seven Last Plagues (Revelation 5, 13, 15). The Caduceus is especially related to the strange Book with Seven Seals, which "no man in heaven, nor in earth, neither under the earth, was able to open and to loose the seals thereof, neither to look thereon" (Revelation 5: 1-4).

The Globe, surmounting the upright Staff, represents man's head. The Wings have a dual significance, representing the Air and also the Mind, which the great Dr. Carrel called, "The most colossal power in this world," and can flash around the world in an instant. The Staff represents the human body, but more especially the Spinal Column.

The Two Serpents of the Staff have puzzled the students of symbolism. One silly fable in the encyclopedias states that as Mercury entered Arcadia, Wand in hand, he saw two serpents locked in combat. He separated them with his Wand, and they immediately coiled around it in friendly union; and so the Wand, with the Serpents, became a Symbol of Peace. More hogwash and hokum for the Man of Darkness.

The Two Serpents represent the great Law of Polarity called the Double Law of Creation by the Ancient Masters. This law explains the universal division of all elements, forces the objects into pairs of opposites, called positive and negative, active and inert, initiative and passive, male and female.

Of this great law one writer said: "The underlying reality which finds ultimate expression in the body of man is the Principle of the Positive and Negative Forces of the Universal Animative Principle, which has produced and does produce all organized forms from the creation of the earth to the creation of man." — The Seventh Seal. A law of such infinite scope must be a law of infinite operation. It appears in the action of all substances, entities, and individuals, which are impelled to unition by the affinities inherent in the elements and objects themselves.

And so the White, Fiery Serpent of the Caduceus and the Black, Evil Serpent indicate the dual powers of Polarity with the Black one ruling the Man of Darkness and the White one governing the Man of Light. These dual forces constantly flow to and fro between mam's brain at the top of the Spinal Cord and the Creative Centers at the base thereof.

In Chapter 4 of Zechariah appears a parable of importance relating to these cosmic forces, and a true and correct interpretation of that parable would surprise the masses. And the angel that talked with me came again and waked me, as a man that is wakened out of his sleep, and said unto me, What seest thou? And I said, I have looked and behold a candlestick all gold (Staff of the Caduceus) with a bowl upon the top of it (human head), and his seven lamps thereon (major nerve ganglia of the spinal cord), and seven pipes to the seven lamps which are upon the top thereof (seven nerve trunks). And two olive trees by it, one upon the right side of the bowl and the other upon the left side thereof (the Two Serpents representing polar force). We are now in the field of profound mysteries of the human body, still unknown to modern science — showing how far ahead of us were the "superstitious heathens" of the prehistoric world.

We shall here simply skim the surface of this deep subject, being unable to do more within the limited space at our disposal. But he who wants the whole story will find it in Hotema's work titled *"Son of Perfection."* We must realize that the body is animated by the Living Fire of the Universe and that the Bible says the "God" of Creation is a "Consuming Fire" (Hebrews 12:29, etc.). The Living Fire is symbolized in the Zodiakos by Aries and Leo.

The negative pole of the Living Fire in the human body is situated at the lower end of the spine, between the last vertebra and the coccyx, while the positive pole is situated just above the atlas, where the head swivels on the spine. It has recently been determined that there are three different forces active in the spinal column. Each has a different frequency. Two of them (Medulla and Black Serpent) can be registered and traced by instruments, and one (White Serpent) which, as it nears the Pineal Gland in the brain, is soon beyond the range of all physical instruments.

The positive phase of the Living Fire, symbolized by the White Serpent, increases in vibratory rate so rapidly from the atlas of the spine to the region of the Pineal Gland in the brain that no instrument known has so far been devised that can register its vibrations.

The vibratory rate beyond the region of the base of the nose has never, to our knowledge, been determined; but it is estimated to be billions of cycles per second.

Numerous experience show what the Masters knew that we can control certain functions of the ductless glands and mentally choose whatever combination we want to bring into operation. Laboratory tests on some of these endocrine-operating Triads show that —

In case of the ordinary love cycle — Pituitary, Thymus, and Gonad glands show a definitely physical love on the animal plane; that is the "love angle" cited in story books, presented in drama, and the cause of much of the world's misery. When the unguided, misguided youth begins to bloom and to feel the urge to propagate according to the law of creation, he thinks he's in "love." In such persons the following conditions have been observed:

1.   Pituitary gland: all mental pictures of opposite sex are delicate and beautiful.
2.   Thymus gland: all sensations in region of heart are gentle and loving.
3.   Gonad glands: Sexual organs are stimulated and the urge to copulate appears.

This is a mental state that rises in the brain, largely controlled by the Pituitary and can all be changed in a moment by thought. Science recently discovered what the Masters knew, that the Pituitary governs all physical functions growth, structure, metabolism, chemical compounding, etc., and even the thoughts, emotions, and senses of the body are under the control of the Pituitary, ruled by the Black Serpent, the Evil Serpent of the Bible.

The Thymus governs heart action, sensation, blood pressure, animal love, under control of the Black Serpent of the Caduceus. The Gonads regulate the semen, glycogen, lactic acid, sex urge, and so on, under the direction of the Pituitary, controlled by Black Serpent.

Ordinarily the Function of all the endocrine triads of the body or the cycles on the physical plane (third dimension) are controlled by the Black Serpent. This reveals the reason why the world is filled with hatred and violence and why so little real harmony and peace prevail. That is the animal level.

All the higher, fourth-dimensional, astral activities are under control of the White Serpent, the Good Serpent of the Bible. This fact was known to and used by the "superstitious heathens" of the ancient world; and now this higher knowledge, possessed by some Occultists, is being re-discovered by science, but is carefully kept in the dark. For science does not want it known that this knowledge was possessed by the Ancient Masters. When the function of any one of the glands forming the triad is disturbed, that disturbs the function of the other two. For instance, let one of the parties in the "love action" willfully interrupt the copulative function, and strange things occur in the mental processes.

The beautiful mental picture instantly changes. The loving sensations of the heart (Thymus) turn to anger and disgust, and we can see defects in our "loved" one which before we saw not.

And the copulatory organ of the male relaxes and becomes temporarily useless for the copulative act.

When the Love Cycle is switched over from the Pituitary to the control of the Pineal, a purely mental process, it changes the spectrum colors of these glands.

When the Gonads radiate dark red under control of the Pituitary and Black Serpent, and we mentally switch over to the control of the Pineal and White Serpent (the high Kingdom of Heaven within), the dark red ceases to radiate from the Gonads; and in place of it a light pink, bordering on orange, appears. And so, when we transfer the Love Cycle from the Pituitary to the Pineal by our mental processes, we raise it up from the animalistic level to the anglesite level and change the vibratory plane of the cycle from control of the Black Serpent to that of the White Serpent. That is part of the secret of the transmutation of the Sex Force to Brain Power, made use of by the Masters; and they presented well-balanced physical bodies and strong Astral Entities. They used the higher purpose of these processes, hence their striking wisdom and ability to perform what appears to us as miracles.

When we encounter something that frightens us, the Pituitary, Thyroid, and Medulla of the Suprarenal form a working triad and go into action. The Pituitary directs the sense organs to ascertain the cause of the fright. The Thymus causes increased heart action and the Medulla of the Suprarenal begins pouring more adrenalin into the blood, to condition the body's muscles for the emergency required to flee or to fight.

When the Pituitary has determined that no longer is there anything to fear, the Medulla of the Suprarenal decreases its action and, in its place in the triad, the Pancreas is substituted, but working in harmony with the Parathyroid and the Spleen, forming a grand cycle.

Let us now consider the point where the Neophyte received the marvelous instructions in the Ancient Mysteries. He was taught how to substitute in place of the Pituitary and Black Serpent the Pineal and White Serpent, which created an equipoise and balanced state.

The Neophyte was instructed how to subdue his animalistic passions by raising his Mind from the animalistic level to the high plane of Astralism. For we change the course of our life with Mental Power. As a man thinketh, so is he (Proverbs 23:7). When we lift up the Mind, we lift up the Man, The Bible says, "Be ye transformed by the renewing of your mind" (Romans 12:2).

And — we look not at the things which are seen (physical world) but at the things which are not seen (Kingdom of Heaven within). For the Kingdom of Heaven is not a place in outer space, but a state of mind. (Romans 34:17). The fault is not in the teaching of the Bible, but in its interpretation. When we close our eyes and mentally concentrate upon the great invisible Kingdom within (Luke 17:21), we are praying in our closet as directed in the Bible (Matthew 6:6).

It would be far better for the masses if more emphasis were put upon the Law of Cause and Effect and less upon being "under grace" (Romans 6:14). Of course it is much more pleasing for the masses to believe that being "under grace" "immunizes" them against the operation of the Law of Cause and Effect than to be solidly told that man must reap just as he sows (Galatians 6:7).

All normal persons possess the miraculous powers mentioned, but they are not taught the terrible truth that sexual activity consumes the precious Vital Essence which sustains the brain, thus causing brain deterioration, weakened Mind, and decreased Consciousness, producing a mass of miserable people that fill the insane asylums, with millions more walking the streets of the cities in freedom because they are harmless and supporting medical art because they are so stupid.

When these secrets of biology, physiology, and pathology are mentioned to the "wise" doctors who are believed to be so intelligent, they scorn the knowledge to hide their ignorance.

Science admits and concedes that the body is physical; but, as the Bible teaches, the mysterious Entity that occupies it on the earth plane is truly the Living Fire, the Consuming Fire of the Hebrews (Hebrews 12:29; 1 Corinthians 3:16, etc.)

Physical instruments now reveal that the inner, astral, or fourth dimensional Entity of the body exists on a vibratory level far above that of the body. And still science sticks to its stupid theory that Life is only "the expression of a series of chemical changes" (Osier mod. Med. p. 29, 1907). And so, according to science, when the body ceases to function, that is the end of Man. That is annihilation, extermination, obliteration.

The discoveries of the great Dr. Carrel so provoked him with his absurd theory of Life that he called it "a childish physicochemical conception sin which so many physiologists and physicians still believe" (*Man The Unknown*, p. 108). And that is the gist of the biological and physiological science taught in our schools and medical colleges.

Chapter 5
Logos

What does Logos mean? It means Word, and this Word has been surrounded with as much mystery as God himself. Freemasonry makes a big mystery over the Lost Word. "The mythical history of Freemasonry," says the Masonic Encyclopedia, "informs us that there once existed a WORD of surpassing value and claiming a profound veneration; that this WORD was known to but few; that it was at length lost; and that a temporary substitute for it was adopted."

What was the meaning of the Lost Word? From the same source we quote the answer:

"But as the very philosophy of Masonry teaches us that there can be no death without a resurrection, no decay without a subsequent restoration, on the same principle it follows that the loss of the Word must suppose its eventual recovery. Now, that it is, precisely, that constitutes the myth of the Lost Word and the search for it. ... The WORD therefore may be conceived to be the Symbol of Divine Truth; and all its modifications — the loss, the substitution, and the recovery are but component parts of the mythical symbol which represents a search after truth."

And so, the WORD was the Symbol of DIVINE TRUTH. But that still leaves us in the dark. Words, words, words, but no definite answers. The Ancient Masters understood human nature so well that they knew the masses could be most strongly attracted by secrecy, mystery, complexity — anything that was difficult to understand or that was not even understandable at all. That is the reason why it is so easy to keep the masses in darkness.

Who can explain the mysterious process of Creation? That explanation is so simple that the masses cannot be interested in it. Consider the transformation of invisible vapor to clouds, then to water, then to ice so strong it will sustain the weight of elephants, presenting the surprising spectacle of gigantic animals standing on invisible vapor. Unbelievable but true. So understandable that the masses give it no thought, and yet in that simple phenomena are contained and revealed the great mystery of Creation. Consider the first statement in the John Gospel: "In the beginning was the Word, and the Word was with God, and the Word was God."

Here we are again, back to the WORD. And in the John statement we have the mysterious God cornered. If the Word was God, then God was the Word, and we can discover the nature of God by a scientific analysis of the Word.

And that is Precisely what we propose to do, and it shall be done by a careful, consistent consideration of the ancient philosophy, the Ageless Wisdom, the Wisdom of the Ancient Masters who invented that WORD.

There is one certain symbol that has been found all over the world, in all ancient countries, and in cities built before there were any mountains on the face of the earth.

The Bible mentions a time before the mountains rose (Proverbs 8:25). And the ruins of ancient cities have been found on mountain tops with evidence present to indicate they were built at sea level. One of these cities was found in South America, the ruins of which are now up in the Andes Mountains three miles high; and in the ruins was an image of the Sphinx with a message carved on the wall of the Temple, referring to the Sacred Four.

"The Sacred Four is among the oldest religious conceptions. I found it in the Sacred Inspired Writings of Mu," said Col. James Church ward in his book *The Sacred Symbols of Mu.*

Four is presented in many ways in the Bible and in all ancient scriptures and occult literature. The Holy City is laid Four Square; the mystical White Stone is square, and there are Four Cardinal Points, North, South, East, and West, presided over by the Four Great Angels or Regents.

In his collection of ancient tablets, some over 12,000 years old, discovered in Mexico by Niven, he found written on some of them, "The Sacred Four," the "Four Great Pillars," the "Four Great Architects," the "Four Great Builders," and the "Four Powerful Ones" (*Symbols of Mu,* p. 74).

In the ancient world there was a secret system of worship, termed the Mysteries, to which none were admitted but those who had been selected by preparatory ceremonies called Initiation.

To conceal the secret teachings of the Mysteries from the profane and uninitiated, the Masters invented Words and Symbols to represent the Elements and Processes of Creation.

In the Temples of Initiation, these Words and Symbols were arranged in a long gallery, supported by caryatides in the form of twenty-four Sphinxes, twelve on each side. On each part of the wall between two Sphinxes there were fresco paintings, representing mystical figures and symbols; and as the candidate passed the pictures, he was halted before each one and received appropriate instruction from the Master of Ceremonies. Of all the Words, Symbols, and Pictures presented to the candidate, one of the more impressive and important was the Sphinx, concerning which the great Kabalist Eliphas Levi, in his book *Transcendental Magic* wrote:

"The Universal Key to magical works is that of all ancient religious dogmas — the Key of the Kabalah and the Bible, the Little Key of Solomon.

"This Clavicle, regarded as lost for centuries, has been recovered by us, and we have been able to open the sepulchres of antiquity, to make the dead speak, to behold the monuments of the past in all their glory, to understand the enigmas of the Sphinx, and to penetrate all sanctuaries.

"Among the ancients, the use of this Key (the Lost Word) was permitted to none but the high priests; and even so, its secret was confined only to the flower of the Initiates. ... This was the Key in question: A hieroglyphic and numeral alphabet; expressing by symbols and numbers a series of universal and absolute ideas. ...

"The symbolical tetrad, represented in the (Egyptian) Mysteries of Memphis and Thebes by the Four (Sacred) Forms of the Sphinx, Man, Eagle, Lion, and Bull, corresponded with the (Sacred) Four Elements of antiquity (Fire, Air, Water, and Earth). ...

"These Four Signs, with all their analogies, explain the one (Sacred) WORD (Logos) hidden in all (the ancient) sanctuaries. ... Moreover, the Sacred WORD was never pronounced; it was always spelled and expressed in four words, which are the Four Sacred Words, Hod He Vau He" (usually written J,H,V,H,).

We are now getting God in a mighty tight corner, and we must not let him escape.

The vowelization in the Bible of the initial letters of the Lost WORD, J.H.V.H., was another clever method employed by the biblical makers to conceal from the profane and uninitiated the secret of the Sacred Four. It is one of many such instances in the Bible which we could indicate, and there are more we have not yet mentioned in our writings.

For instance, in Revelation an important case of this kind is the statement: "And he has a name written that no man knew but he himself. And he was clothed with a vesture dipped in blood; and his name is called The Word of God" (Revelation 19:12,13).

This is the Initiate of the Ancient Mysteries symbolized by the Blazing Star of Bethlehem, signifying that he has subdued his passions, conquered his lower animal nature (killed his beasts says the Bible — Proverbs 9:2), and completed the elastic work, after which he was set apart from the profane and exoteric by being clad in a special garment dyed red; and his name was now called THE SON OF LIGHT, being no longer the inverted man of darkness symbolized by the Black Pentacle. We shall go on and notice verse 10, same chapter of Revelation, in which appears the statement, "For the TESTIMONY of JESUS is the SPIRIT OF PROPHECY."

Here again appears the clever work of the biblical makers in concealing the Ageless Wisdom from the profane and exoteric. When properly presented, that statement reads, "For the EVIDENCE of RESURRECTION (of the Living Fire from the base of the spine up to the brain) is the POWER OF SEERSHIP." One of the principal objectives of initiation was to teach the Neophyte the physiological secret of activating the semi-dormant Pituitary and Pineal glands of the brain by conserving the Living Fire of Creation at the base of the spine (grave) so it would rise up and flow to the brain (heaven).

That is the secret meaning of the statement in the Bible, "She hath killed her beasts" (Proverbs 9:2). This was one of the golden secrets of the Masters. That exalted state is symbolized in ancient sculpture by the head of a Serpent, protruding from man's forehead and indicating the activation of the mysterious Third Eye, mentioned in the Bible as the Single Eye that fills the whole body with Light (Matthew 6:22). This vital psychic center in the brain, termed the Trikona by the Masters, was said to be the Throne of Astral Intelligence. By the activation and mastery of this psychic center, we are told that one is able to overcome the Karma of one's antecedent incarnations and to rise above the element of Time-Space, as in dreams. And for such, the Past and Future merge and become the Eternal Present.

We are also told that as the Living Fire, Serpentine Fire, Kundalini, flows up the spinal cord, there is a golden glow radiating outward from a fine line of what appears as a stream of Yellow Fire. The color extends somewhat outward along the nerves that branch off from the spinal cord between the vertebrae. The last book of the Bible, in heavily veiled allegory, is devoted exclusively to this precious secret of the Masters; and the ascension of the Living Fire up the spinal cord is traced three times in the allegory. In the first instance, there is given a general description of the areas of the body primarily affected by the activation of the nerve centers controlling those areas.

In the second, a brief sketch is given of the effect of this increased activity in each of the seven principal nerve centers, as they are stimulated by the ascension of the Living Fire from the spinal base. In the third, there is presented in an ingenious fable, termed "The Seven Last Plagues" (Revelation 15), the deeper sensations experienced by the Neophyte of the increased activity in each part of the body, as the ascending Fire Of Life activates the Seven Principal Nerve Centers of the body, which is called in the allegory the Book With Seven Seals (Rev. 5).

The last and greatest effect in the psycho-bio-physiological processes is the striking activation by the Living Fire of the semi-dormant Pituitary and Pineal glands of the brain, the great organs of Premonition and Clairvoyance — the Powers of Seership, and, in the allegory termed "The marriage of the Lamb" (Revelation 19:7), the details of which Hotema explains in his work titled Son of Perfections. Such men were called the Sons of Light in the ancient scriptures and also the Sons of God. Those of this special class constituted the higher element that was not "given in marriage, but are (free of carnal lust) as the angels in heaven" (Matthew 22:30).

And so we perceive that the baffling allegories of the Bible cleverly unfold into strange, scientific knowledge of Man when properly interpreted. These allegories are the work of Master Scientists in the subjects of Anthropology, Biology, Psychology, and Physiology, standing high above the greatest scientist of this age who are lost in darkness because, in their consideration of Man, they refuse to go beyond the narrow limit of what the great Dr. Carrel called the "childish physico-chemical conceptions of human beings" (*Man The Unknown,* p. 108).

To conceal its ignorance, modern science sneers the suggestion that beyond such limit there exists the Infinite, Universal Animative Principle which is not only the CAUSE of the physico-chemical action, but definitely controls it. This means that, by its own work, modern science creates the darkness in which it is lost. And as we take another look at the Bible, we observe, as we might well expect, that some of the high class of Initiates weakened mentally and became "backsliders." For they looked and "saw the (beautiful) daughters of men (who were not Initiates) that they were fair; and they took them wives of all which they chose" (Genesis 6:2). That particular phase of this subject is covered by the symbolism of Card No. 6 of the ancient Tarot, titled "Temptation," and in the Bible by chapters 2 and 3 of Genesis, in which is allegorically taught one of the great lessons of life, yet passed over by the Clergy as a subject too delicate for discussion. Our level of knowledge is low and mode of living is lower if we blush with shame when the Facts of Creation are properly presented to us.

And now we come to that great Logos, the mysterious Lost WORD. Among the Hebrews this was the Ineffable Name, consisting of the letters J.H.V.H., and referred to the Sacred Four represented by the Sphinx, a strange image the real meaning of which is a mystery to the modern world. He who understood this secret knew the facts of the mysterious unition of God with all His Creation. And that was a secret which the Masters wanted to conceal from all but the Initiates.

Various methods were employed by the biblical makers to hide from the profane and exoteric, the secrets of the Ageless Wisdom which were reserved strictly for those who proved by their work that they were worthy to receive the same. And as we proceed to reveal that profound secret, the majority of the masses will simply turn up their noses and continue to search for the mysterious and complex.

The study of the Ineffable Name in all its manifestations and various variations constituted the basis of the great Kabalah. The four letters, J.H.V.H., were given a symbolical meaning. The first expressed the active principle, unitiative; the second, the passive principle, inertia; the third, equilibrium, "form," and the fourth, result of latent energy. The Kabalists affirmed that every phenomena and every object consists of the Sacred Word, the Word that was in the beginning, the Word that was with God, and the Word was God.

The study of it and the finding of it in everything constituted the chief aim of Kabalistic philosophy. There was much-to-do about something that is very simple. According to the Kabalists, the Sacred Four Elements permeate and compose each and every thing and object known and unknown. Hence, by finding these Four Elements in objects and phenomena of quite different categories, between which man had previously seen nothing in common, the man on the earth and the moon in the sky for instance, he began to discover the analogy between these objects and gradually grew convinced that everything in the world is constructed of the Four Elements according to the same law and the same plan.

The principle is obvious: If the Logos, the Lost Word, the In-effable Name, J.H.V.H., *is* in everything, if the Sacred Word appears in everything, then everything should be analogous to everything else, the smallest part should be analogous to the whole, the speck of dust analogous to the Universe and all analogous to God. "As above, so below."

And there is the golden secret of the mysterious Word that was in the beginning, the Word which was with God, and the Word was God.

Speculative philosophy arrives at the conclusion that the world undoubtedly exists but that our conception of it is erroneous. The causes of our sensations, which are external to us, really exist; but our conception of them is deceptive. In other words, the world in itself, by itself, without our perception of it, really exists, but we do not know it and can never reach it with our common Five Senses, for all that is accessible to our study is only our illusive perception of the world. The Kabalah aims at studying the world as it actually is, the world in itself. The other ancient, mystical sciences had the same objective.

In Alchemy, the Sacred Four Elements of which the world consists are called fire, air, water, and earth, which correspond in their meaning to the four letters J.H.V.H.

In the Bible they are presented as the Four Beasts before the throne, one like lion, the second like a calf, the third was the face of a man, and the fourth like a flying eagle (Revelation 14:6, 7).

And all these combined are the mysterious Sphinx, the symbol of the Sacred Four merged into one form. And this image is stupidly mentioned in the encyclopedias as "A mythological monster, variously described and, in the mythology of ancient Egypt, represents the Solar diety Ra."

So, God created man in his own image, in the image of God, after his likeness, God created man (Genesis 26, 27). The CREATED must resemble the CREATOR in character if not in degree.

The CREATED is composed of Fire, Air, Water, and Earth, and so is the CREATOR. These elements are the Sacred Four, and the ancient symbol of the Sacred Four is J.H.V.H. and the constitution of the Sacred Four are Fire, Air, Water, aid Earth. And that is one of the great mysteries of the Ancient Masters. It was arranged as a Mystery to arouse the interest of the Initiates and to produce the confusion and curiosity of the masses. Very clever, very skillfully, very effective.

No wonder that it took eighty years to make the first copy of the Bible from the Ancient Scrolls. It required lots of time to take the greatest philosophy of Life and arrange it in words, phrases, and sentences which would conceal the true essence of the teachings so well and so completely that it required years of labor in the study of ancient literature for one to acquire the knowledge necessary to interpret the writings in the Bible and dig out the hidden meaning of the messages.

Chapter 6
The Living Fire

"To the God Who is in the Fire" (Shivat Upanishad).

"For our God is a Consuming Fire" (Hebrews 12:29, etc.).

"I sense one Flame; O Gurudeva; I see countless undetached sparks shining in it" (*Secret Doctrine*, Blavatsky).

"The Esoteric Teaching sayeth that Fire is the perfect and un-adulterated reflection in Heaven as on Earth of the One Divine Flame. It is Life and Death, the origin and the end of every material thing. It is Divine Substance" (S.D., Blavatsky).

"There is one Boundless, Immutable Principle; one Absolute Reality which antecedes all manifested conditioned Being. It is beyond the range and reach of human thought or expression" (*Treatise on Cosmic Fire* by Alice Bailey).

"The Secret of Fire lieth hid in the second letter of the Sacred Word (J.H.V.H.). When the lower point vibrates, when the sacred Triangle glows, when the point, the middle center and the apex, connect and circulate the Fire, when the threefold apex likewise Flames, then the Two Triangles (the Blazing and the Black), the greater and the lesser, merge into one Flame, which consumed the whole" (S.D. Blavatsky).

Said Clymer, "Fire, indeed, would seem to be the chosen element of God. ... All the early Fathers considered the Creator to appear as 'subtle Fire.'.... The primary Scriptural Type of the Father is Fire. "Fire Philosophy is the foundation of all religion; it is the philosophy of the Soul and of God.

Without Fire and the resultant heat, there could be no existence. God and the Soul are One and the same thing — The Living Fire" (Dr. R.S. Clymer, *Philosophy of Fire.*).

In the year 1881, there was made a surprising discovery. Excavation in Babylonia unearthed a clay chest, among other treasures found, which contained an artistically inscribed alabaster tablet in six volumes, decorated at the top with a skill fully executed bas-relief.

In this Holy of Holies there was seated upon a Throne decorated with cherubim, a god with flowing beard. In his hand a ring, symbol of Eternity, and a staff (Caduceus, symbol of the Creative Principle). A king, followed by two priests, approaches the god in adoration, while two other men are raising the Sun Disk with ropes upon the roof of the Holy of Holies.

A valuable discovery, but more so because the tablet also revealed the name of the building and of the city thus discovered — "Image of the Sun God, the Great Lord, who dwells in the Temple of Ebabbars in the City of Sippar."

One of the most ancient of Babylonian cities had been discovered in which Noah-Kisusthros, by command of the God Kronos, was ordered to bury the tablets of antediluvian days. The Sun Temple, which since its foundation long after the time of the last Chaldean King, was the center of worship for the Babylonians; and so, the subject of concern of all Babylonian Kings was re-discovered. The treasures found take us way back and open a vista into the past history of humanity on Babylonian soil, extending far beyond the time of Abraham, whose story begins with the 12th chapter of Genesis. In the Bible the Psalmist sings a lyric unto the Sun, the Monad or First Form emanating from the Almighty: --

"The Lord reigneth; let the earth rejoice; let the multitude of isles be glad. Clouds and darkness round about Him; righteousness and judgment the habitation of His throne. A fire goeth before Him, and burneth up His enemies round about Him. His lightning's enlightened the world; the earth saw and trembled. The hills melted like wax at the presence of the Lord. ...The heavens declare His righteousness, and all the people saw His glory" (Psalms 97: 1-6).

The Living Fire of the Ancient Masters was the leading philosophy of the ancient world; and now it lies buried beneath the ruins of the Temples of antiquity. Fragments thereof are preserved in the Bible and in various other works of ancient lore. In the humblest hut in the East there is always a light that never fails, physically nor symbolically. A light constantly burns before the Holy Ark of the Synagogue; also one over the altar of the Church, and one illuminates the Crescent of the Mosque. In ancient days there was always a light upon the hearth.

The word Pyramid comes from the Greek Pry, which means Fire or Light that illuminates and heats, and Midas, which means "measures." And so Pyramid means Light Measures.

The great Pyramid of Gizehl built forty thousand years ago some authors claim, symbolized the Terrestrial Flame, the White Triangle representing the Microcosm, seeking ascension to the absorption in the Celestial Flame, the Macrocosm. The Fire Philosophers held that we transcend everything into Fire. All things are derived from Fire by rarefaction and condensation, the one active and the other passive, the one synthetic and the other analytic.

Heraclitus (535-475 B.C.) taught that as all things are derived from Fire, they are eventually transformed again to Fire. For consistency of thought demands that we proceed in our processes in a direct line thru infinite time to infinite results. The Ancient Astrologers said, "From Fire to Earth and back again, an infinite number of worlds are born, only to suffer annihilation in due course, succeeded by reconstruction and re-destruction without end. In a word, the entire Universe is "Fire in the process of transformation."

The Pythagoreans considered Fire as constituting the Heart of the Universe. They regarded Fire as extending from the earth to the limits of the Cosmos. All things are derived from Fire and strive ever to return to Fire, the Eternal Flame Divine. Ancient

Science attributed to Fire a far wider connotation than it has for us. All solids are condensed Fire, only to be rekindled in the process of universal transformation.

The great Kabalist Eliphas Levi wrote:

"All Assyrian symbols (are) connected with this Science of Fire, which was the great secret of the Magi. On every side we meet with the enchanter who slays the lion and controls the serpents. That lion is (a symbol of) the Celestial Fire, while the serpents are (symbols of) the electric (positive} and magnetic (negative) currents of the earth. To this same great secret of the Magi are referable all marvels of Hermetic Magic, the extant traditions of which still bear witnesses that the mystery of the Great Work consists in the ruling of Fire (Hist. of Mag., P. 66).

Dr, E. A. Waite quoted from an ancient work on Fire as follows: "When thou dost behold the very sacred Fire with dancing radiance, flashing formless thru the depths of the world, then harken to the Voice of Fire" (p, 67). Manly Hall wrote: "There is but one religion in all the world, and that is the worship of God, the Spiritual Flame of the Universes Under many names He is known in all lands, but whether as Ishwar, or Ammon, or God, He is ever the same — the Creator of the Universe, the Fire is His universal symbol" (Initiates of the Flame, p. 14). Fire is the most ancient symbol of Life and the greatest of all purifying agencies known. In the Egyptian Mysteries there was a symbolical purification of the Neophyte by the Sacred Fire. The purifying power of Fire is logically deducted from its symbol of the holiness of the Sacred Four Elements. And in the high degree of Masonry, as in the ancient Temples, there is a purification by Fire, coming down to us insensibly and unconsciously from the ancient Magi. As Fire and Light are identical, so Fire was, to the ancient Magi, the Symbol of the Creator.

The initials I.N.R.I. of the Latin sentence which appears upon the Cross, and is translated Jesus Nazarenus Rex

Judaeorum, were used by the Rosicrucians as the initials of one of their Hermetic secrets: "Inge Nature Renovator Integra" (by Fire, Nature is perfectly renewed). They are also the initials of the Hebrew names of the Sacred Four Creative Elements: Iaminim (water), Nour (fire), Ruach (air), and Iebschah (earth).

Jennings Hargrave stated in his book that what had been assumed to be a tomb in the center of the Great Pyramid was in reality a depository of the Sacred Fire.

The Flashing Flame darting upward to meet its divine original, the Terrestrial Fire seeking ascension to the absorption in the Celestial Fire, or God, constituted what has been called the Flame Secret of the Fire Worshippers. This most ancient religion passed from the now sunken continent Lemuria to India, thence to Egypt, Asia Minor, Judea, Greece, and Rome.

The God of Fire appeared unto Moses in a Flame of Fire. He desended upon Mount Sinai in the midst of Flames. Everywhere in the Scriptures, Fire is a symbol of God, and Fire was venerated as a visible symbol of the Supreme Deity. Fire and Light were the uniform tokens of the appearances of the Deity. Sometimes shining with a mild and gentle radiance, like the interior luminaries of a Light on the Altar, and at others flaming fiercely admist clouds and darkness rumblings and thunderings.

To Adam He appeared in the Shekinah, which kept the gates of Paradise; to Abel and Enoch and Noah, the Deity appeared in a Flame of Fire. And in like manner unto Abraham, Isaac, and Jacob.

What is Light? We no more know than did the ancients. According to the modern hypothesis, it is not composed of luminous particles shot from the sun with terrific velocity. That body only impresses upon the substance which fills all space, a powerful vibratory movement that extends, in the form of luminous waves, beyond the most distant planets, supplying them with light and heat.

It is not strange that, thousands of years ago, men worshipped the Sun. But they looked beyond the orb to the invisible God of whom the Sun's light, seemingly the cause of generation and life, was the manifestation and out flowing. Long ages before the Chaldean shepherds watched the Sun on their plains, it rose regularly, as it does now, in the morning, like a god, and again sank in the west like a retiring king, to return again in due time in the same array of majesty. We admire immutability, and it was that regular, constant, immutable quality of the Sun that the Ancient Masters worshipped.

The Living Fire of the world, motive power of the Universe, was held by the Masters to exercise its creative energy chiefly thru the agency of the Sun, during its revolution along the signs of the Zodiakos, with which signs unite the paranatallons that modify their influence, and concur in finishing the symbolic attributes of the Great Luminary that regulates all Nature and is the depositary of all universal powers.

Atomistic Eschatology

In 1917 Dr. Robert A. Millikan, the generalissimo of American Science in World War I, said that "Thales, as far back as 600 B.C., correctly conceived and correctly stated the gist of that which has actually guided science in the development of physics in all ages." Thales held that the First Principle is not only the cause of Matter and Motion, but is Matter and Motion combined.

Anaximander and Anaximines followed in succession in the tracks of Thales. Anaximines advanced the hypothesis that Air (AER) is the First Principle of all cosmic phenomena and that "all things are generated by a certain condensation and rarefaction of Air." He said:

"Air is the nearest to an immaterial substance; for since we are generated in the flow of air, it is necessary that air should be infinite and limitless because it is never exhausted." And he held that Air is an animate substance, in constant motion, and is thus constantly changing forms, generating new things — things not contained, as such, in the primitive homogeneous substance.

When very much attenuated, Air becomes Fire; when more condensed, wind; a still further condensation produces clouds; greater compression changes clouds to water; further pressure produces the earth; and finally stones are formed as Matter becomes still more condensed; these successive changes being brought about by motion, which is continuous and eternal.

It was considered that Force is an inherent attribute of the primordial living substance; hence Air is, for Anaximines, the Creative Cause of the world and all it contains. Thus have all things cone into existence and thus shall be generated, "all the things that will be."

As this postulate provided no place for a God of Creation, the writings of Anaximines were ruthlessly destroyed by the Church, and it is surprising that even one single fragment survived.

When modern science began to bud some centuries ago, Matter was considered as something solid and opposite to Force. But that scientific postulate got a big shock with the cracking of the atom. Camille Flammarion wrote: "Matter is not all that it seems to be to our senses, to touch, or vision. ... It represents one single whole with energy and is the manifestation of the motion of the invisible and imponderable elements.

Recent discoveries show that what we see and call matter is delusion. It is a state, not and object. And that state is produced by the vortexial whorls of Force resolved in space into orbits and confined to these orbits by cosmic law which alters not Dr. David J. Calicchio says: "There is a strange law that binds together all the diverse elements of Matter" (Electronlogy, p. 11).

Science declares that if the vortexial motion of all the apparent solid substance in or on the earth were arrested, the resultant mass of Matter could be collected in a ball no bigger than an ordinary pumpkin. The infinitesimal rotating particles of the atom which appear to give the atom form are relatively as far apart as the sun is from the earth with apparently nothing but space in between. Our Sun, composed of highly revolving specks of gas and establishing radiations of vibration that move with the velocity of light, contains less solid matter per cubic mile than the earth.

Igneology

We shall see what science knows about Fire by referring to the encyclopedias. The Americana, 1938 edition, says:

"The terrific energy of fire, the most important agent of civilization, the similarity of its effects with that of the sun, its intimate connection with light, its terrible and yet genial power, and the beauty of its changeful flame easily account for the reverence in which it was held in ancient times.

"At a period when cause and effect, form and essence, were not distinctly separated, fire became an object of religious veneration, a distinguished element in mythology, an expressive symbol in poetry and an important agent in the systems of cosmogony. It gained a Place among the elements, and for a long time it was believed to be a constituent part in the composition of all bodies. At a later period, fire, under the name of phlogiston, was considered to be the source of all chemical action" (Vol. 11, p. 232). The absurdity of that statement and the stupidity of the hand that wrote it will grow more apparent as we proceed.

The essential principle of the theory of phlogiston was that combustion is a decomposition rather than a union and combination, which it has since shown to be. But that still leaves us in the dark, so far as science is concerned, as to the exact nature of Fire,

When the Ancient Masters said, "For our God is a Consuming Fire" (Hebrews 12:29, etc.), what did they have in mind when they were too "dumb and ignorant" to separate cause and effect, form and essence? They were not thinking of phlogiston or decomposition or chemical action. They had in mind Principles and Causes, not Effects and Results. Reraclitus (535 - 75 B.C.) held that thruout the Universe there exists a prime substance which he called Fiery Ether.

Long before him, the Ignicolists called it Astral Light. Modern science calls it Cosmic Radiation. Dr. Velikovsky called it Electo-Magnetism, an element unknown to the great Isaac Newton (Earth In Upheaven). Dr. Calicchio called it Electricity and said:

"Everything in existence (everything known and unknown) consists of Electricity. ...The entire Universe is moved by the positive and negative forces of electrical action. And all operations of nature in and on the earth and its elements are carried on by the same force.

"Whether it be crystallization or disintegration, the growth of vegetables or their decomposition or the crumbling particles of mountain rock, all motion visible and invisible that transpires in the mineral, vegetable, and animal kingdoms, in all their multifarious operations are produced by electricity, which is the universal agent that keeps up the harmony and order of the Universe" (Electronology). Cosmic Electricity is the Ultimation, the Fire appears as its active state.

Ignification changes every known substance into a state of electricity that vanishes from sight as invisible gas; and there goes that solid, material world of our scientists. Dr. J. H. Haldane, great astronomer, said:

"Materialism, once a plausible theory, is now the fatalistic creed of thousands, but materialism is nothing better than a superstition, on the same level as a belief in witches and devils. The materialist theory if bankrupt."

Matter, physical substance, is condensed fire or condensed electricity; and the degrees of condensation extend in regular order from the densest substances known, such as stone and steel, to the rarest, called "Fiery Ether."

Electricity is the element of which are constituted all the suns, stars, planets, moons, objects, and organisms. It is the element that binds together the diverse elements of matter. It is inextricable network of vibrations, waves, and influences, or nameless, numberless, and uninterrupted fluids that connect everything with everything that exists.

Electricity is the cosmic element that has never been clearly defined. Nor has it been clearly recognized for what it is. Science shows that it exists primarily in two distinct forms- concentrated in the form of electrons and protons and waves classed as radiation.

The electron is the smallest known particle having a negative charge capable of isolation and measurement. The proton has a positive charge, the numerical value of the charge being equal to the electronic charge. The atom has as many extra nuclear electrons as there are protons in its nucleus; and as the positive charge of the proton equals numerically the negative charge carried by each electron, the atom as a whole is electrically neutral. That is equilibrium. And when that equilibrium is disturbed, the fire flies.

This fact may be demonstrated by the electric battery in an automobile. The battery is electrically neutral until its negative and positive poles are properly connected. Then, by pressing the button, its equilibrium is disturbed; and the result is a stream of invisible fire that starts the motor of the car. That stream of fire is the active state of electricity. Combustion is a state of burning in which matter is transmuted to cosmic electricity in the form of invisible gas. That is demonstrable proof that matter or substance is condensed electricity. Then it logically follows that everybody, every object, is constituted of condensed electricity, including the flesh and bones of the human body.

Decay is a slower process of disintegration, but the ultimate product is the same — cosmic electricity, which appears in the form of dust that finally changes to invisible gas.

And so the atom, formerly regarded by science as indivisible, is now recognized as complex, composed of electrons and protons as stated. These are not material particles in the usual sense of the word. They are better defined as moments of manifestation of force, moments or elements of force. To state it in other words, electrons and protons, representing the smallest divisions of matter possible, are at the same time the smallest divisions of force.

It is possible to think that the difference between matter and force consists simply in the different combinations of positive and negative particles. In one combination they produce on our senses the impression of matter and in another the impression of force. From this point of view, the difference between force and matter, which constitutes so far the basis of our view of cosmic phenomena, does not exist. It is imaginary.

Force and matter are two aspects of the same element, or the different manifestations of one and the same thing. There is no essential difference between force and matter, and the one must pass into the other. Electricity, the exact nature of which is still unknown, but which was better understood by the Ancient Masters than by us, appears in different forms, concentrated as particles of matter called electrons and protons, or in rapid motion as light, radiation, radio-telegraph waves, etc. Heraclitus said the factor called Life is "a portion of Universal Fire (Electricity) imprisoned in a body constituted of water and earth," and that water and earth are condensed electricity.

And so, the Hebrews said that all things are the progeny fire; "For our God is a Consuming Fire" (Hebrews 12:29, etc.) And it is law that the Created must resemble the Creator in character if not in degree. "As above, so below."

The fundamental doctrine of the ancient religion of India and Persia was the veneration of the Sacred Fire and above all, Light — Air, not the lower atmospheric air, but the purer and brighter Air of the Celestial World, the Vital Breath that animates and pervades the Breath of Mortal Life.

The Fiery Man

In his work titled *The Flame Divine*, Hotema has given the world surprising description of the Fiery Man. Various authors write about the physical body, casual body, astral body, etherical body, and spiritual body; but none seem to have discovered the Solarical Body, the Electrical Body, the Ignifical Body. They may have heard of the Spark of Life but did not appreciate the profound significance of the term. Hotema tells in *The Flame Divine* that a pin cannot penetrate the flesh anywhere without drawing fluid from the body, which is composed of blood and lymph; and these are liquefied air. The bony frame of the body, the densest part, is built by the blood, of blood, making the bones solidified blood, which is composed of liquefied air.

These subdivisions combined constitute physical man. They are composed of condensed air, which is composed of incandescent gases, which are composed of atoms, making the body an aggregation of atoms. Interpenetrating, engendering, sustaining, vitalizing, and intelligizing these divisions of the body is the mysterious work of the most powerful, most inexplicable, and most dangerous Force known, called by the Ancient Masters the Consuming Fire.

A pin cannot be pressed against the body anywhere without touching a Nerve; and, during the life of the body, the Nerves are charged with what science calls Nerve Force.

For this force science has no definite name nor explanation. It may be "food energy," resulting from "chemical action" in the body or "a series of chemical changes occurring in the cells," as the great Osier said. This Nerve System, composed of vito-electrical wires, constitutes the Electrical Man. The wires are interlaced, interwove, and interblended so completely and so perfectly with every part of the physical body that in our sight the Electrical Man and his physical body appear as one. And so, when we gaze in a mirror, we see only the physical form, but we are actually looking at the Eternal Solar or Electrical Man.

We shall refer to the Bible again in order to show the reader how far ahead of us were the Ancient Masters. The Bible mentions the silver Cord, Jacob's Ladder, and "a door opened in heaven," but to the preachers this symbolism means nothing.

1.   *Or ever the Silver Cord be loosed, or the Golden Bowl be broken* (Ecclesiastics 12:6).
2.   *And Jacob dreamed, and behold a ladder set up on the earth, and the top of it reached to heaven; and the angels (were) ascending and descending on it* (Genesis 28:12).
3.   *After this I looked and, behold, a door (was) opened in heaven* (Revelations 4:1).

Science never dreams that this strange symbolism conceals from the eyes of the world certain creative processes of the Universe and definite animative functions in the human body.

We now come to a strange secret. The nerves, say medical books, begin in the brain and end in various parts and organs of the body. If that were a fact, the vitality, consciousness, mind, and intelligence of man would be the greatest of all mysteries and miracles.

These are the qualities of Life, and these are such a puzzle to our smug science that no concerted effort is made to analyze them. There seems to be no place to begin. Our great scientists frankly admit that they cannot define Life nor explain why they are alive.

Now, if the nerves do begin in the brain, whence comes the strange, inexplicable power called "nerve force," which science says animates the body, makes all parts of the body to function and the heart to beat? No sound, sensible, logical, scientific answer to that big question is contained in all the medical books on earth. Medical art has not solved the very first problem of Life. Science knows little about the nerves and nothing about the essence of "nerve force."

The nerves just begin in the brain; and mind, consciousness, intelligence, vitality, and nerve force originate in the brain. From what? These qualities which constitute Life just seem to spring from nothing or to rise from internal chemical action.

The nerves appear to begin in the brain, but do not. The sun seems to rise, but does not. The earth seems to be stationary, but is not. When Dr. Wm. Harvey shocked the medical world in 1616 with the announcement of his discovery of the circulation of the blood in the body, he could not determine how the blood passes from the arteries to the veins, as no connecting tubes could be seen by the aid of the best microscope available. Harvey knew the blood passes from the arteries to the veins, but he could not explain the mystery. The arteries seem to end in nothing and the veins to begin in nothing. Just as the nerves seem to begin from nothing in the brain.

Medical art, learning nothing from that experience, says the nerves begin in the brain, converge at the Medulle Oblongata portion of the brain, and there form the spinal cord, which extends down the spine, with nerves branching from it and going all over the body.

The Ancient Masters knew that the nerves could not begin in the brain; for the nerves are charged with a Fiery Force that does not originate in the brain and is not generated in the body. Now for an amazing secret: The brain and nerves of the body are condensed Astral Rays.

Astral Rays, called Astral Light by the Ancient Masters, converge as the Silver Cord at the Fonticulus Frontalis (door opened in heaven) in the crown of the head (Golden Bowl) and there transform by condensation into material substance forming the brain and the nerve system. This is the Electrical Body. In 1953, two Canadian doctors demonstrated by test that the leaves of sugar beets changed cosmic rays into cellulose in ten seconds. Lead, a metallic substance, when put in a pot on a hot stove, soon melts and boils away and floats in the air as invisible gas. Ice is solidified vapor. As the leaves of beets change astral rays into cellulose, 30 astral rays condense into brain substance and nerve fibers. In the formative stage of the embryo, the brain forms first by the condensation of astral rays.

The skull area where the Silver Cord penetrates the Golden Bowl is the Fonticulus Frontalis. To this important fontanel no medical book pays any especial attention. If it has a particular purpose, medical art knows it not. In the skull there are seven fontanels. This one is much the largest, remains open for a considerable time after birth, and presents a rhythmic pulsation that accords with the heart's beat.

We are now at the core of the Fiery Essence of the Universe that flows into the body, producing the state we call Life. This Macrocosmic Current contains the Virility of all Life and flows into the brain and body as the Silver Cord. This is the mysterious Animative Force for which medical art has vague theories but no definite explanation. Whence comes the force responsible for the psychological, biological, and physiological processes of the body? Whence come the inexplicable qualities called vitality, mind, consciousness, and intelligence? For these profound questions medical art has no answer. They may come from the brain or from the food one eats. And that stupid system of speculation is called "medical science."

The Microcosm is of and from the Macrocosm, and the rhythmic pulsation and properties of the Macrocosm appear in the Microcosm. Doctors wonder as they witness the rhythms of cosmic force, but see not that the same rhythms appear in all physical processes of the body, nor realize that they are the expressions of that vito-electro-essence of the Macrocosm which makes the Microcosm a Living Soul.

Chapter 7
Secret of Life

The Ageless Wisdom taught the secret of Life and explained the mysterious door opened in heaven (Revelation 4:1), the Silver Cord, Golden Bowl (Ecclesiastics 12:6), and Jacobs Ladder (Genesis 28:12).

Hotema said in *The Flame Divine* that the Silver Cord and Golden Bowl are mentioned so casually in the Bible that people think they may refer to jewelry and ornaments. No one would think the Silver Cord had any relation to a creative process or that the Golden Bowl signified a certain part of the human body.

The Silver Cord is the cosmic cable of Astral Radiation that links the Physical Man with the Astral Man. It lowers the Astral Man into his physical prison, where he hangs on the symbolical cross for evil purposes, with his days filled with lust and sensation, greed, hate, jealousy, etc.

Then, when his miseries and sufferings in his physical prison on earth are ended in the "Born Again" process called Death, the Silver Cord lifts him up to his eternal home in the Celestial Realm, thru the "door opened in heaven."

And so, the angels descending and ascending on Jacob's Ladder represent the journey of man, descending into the physical world in the cosmic process called Birth and ascending to the astral world in the "Born Again" process called Death. Unknown to science, the Silver Cord and Spinal Cord are actually a continuation of each other, the Spinal Cord being the material extension of the Silver Cord.

At the lower end of the Spinal Cord in the human body is the Creative Power of the Microcosm; and at the upper end of the Silver Cord in the astral world is the Cosmic Creative Power of the Macrocosm.

Astral Radiation, flowing as the Silver Cord from the Astral World, is the mysterious Nerve Force, Vital Force, Life Force. It could be called Cosmic Radiation or Cosmic Vibration and is the cause of the beating of the heart, the flowing of the blood, and all the pulsation of the body, glands, organs, and cells. This mysterious force does not originate in the body or in the brain as science claims. And those who call it the Life Principle are in error, as there is no Life Principle, except in name only. What we call Life is only body function, and the power responsible for that function is the great mystery.

The mystery of leaving the body in death is described by one who recovered from a death-like swoon and who says it is like struggling thru a dark, narrow tunnel into a big, brightly illuminated space. How similar to being born in the flesh. The typical experience of the infant during the time immediately after being born of the mother. And, in the cosmic process of dying, the Mind grows clearer than ever before in earthly life; and the head, the Golden Bowl, becomes intensely brilliant.

The Silver Cord also grows stronger to protect the Ego, the Astral Man; and "the etheric body," says one author, "flows out (of the Fonticulus Frontalis in the top of the head) thru the Silver Cord like a rapidly moving fluorescent light, imperceptibly extracting the body's vitality, somewhat as a suction pump; and the Ego leaves the body thru the top of the head as an Astral Light that may be seen by a true clairvoyant.

And that is a scientific description of the dreaded, terrifying physiological process of dying, the "Born Again" mystery, whichis all over, says the Bible, "in the twinkling of an eye" (1 Corinthians 15:52).

Chapter 8
Gods Law of Life

The true Science of Health and Economics rests upon the Five Basic and Eternal Principles of God's Fundamental Plan of Life. These principles are recorded in the Bible as follows, to-wit:

1. *GOD PLANTED A GARDEN EASTWARD IN EDEN (TROPICAL INDIA) AND THERE put MAN* (Genesis 2:8).
   That statement indicates man's natural environment. That phase of the law has not changed. Man has changed his environment, and for so doing he pays a bitter penalty.
2. *IN THE (TROPICAL) GARDEN GREW EVERY TREE THAT IS PLEASANT TO THE SIGHT AND GOOD FOR FOOD* (Genesis 2:9).
   That statement indicates man's natural diet. That phase of the law has not changed. Man has changed his diet, and for so doing he pays a bitter penalty.
3. *THE GARDEN HAD A NATURAL WATER SUPPLY, AMPLE FOR ALL PURPOSES, FURNISHED BY FOUR RIVERS* (Genesis 2:10-14).
   The law makes no provision for artificial irrigational systems. It was not intended that ants food, and even his life, should depend on such dangerous and uncertain things as artificial irrigation systems.
4   *MAN'S APPOINTED WORK WAS TO DRESS THE GARDEN AND TO KEEP IT* (Genesis 2:15).
   That statement points out man's natural labor. That phase of the law has not changed. Man has changed his work, and now millions of men wear away their lives in artificial sweat-shops. For so doing man pays a bitter penalty.

5. *THE CLIMATE OF THE GARDEN WAS THAT OF PERPETUAL SUMMER. FOR MAN WAS NAKED AND NOT UNCOMFORTABLE* (Genesis 2:25).

That statement shows that God never intended man's life and comfort should depend upon (1) artificial clothing, (2) artificial shelter, and (3) artificial heat.

It is absurd to assert that God, in the might of His wisdom, omitted anything that is essential for man's comfort and welfare. These artificial "necessities of life" arise directly from man's unlawful attempt to change his environment and his mode of living from the natural to the artificial.

From that unlawful act arises the modern economic burden that is crushing man to the earth. There is no relief except obedience to the law.

These Five Eternal Principles constitute God's Fundamental Plan of Life. They constitute the true Science of Health and Economics. They are founded upon Universal Law. They never change. They show the way to the Life that God intended. Those who follow it receive the blessings of Divine Providence.

Climate

No other factor affects the Body so much as Climate. A hostile climate builds a sickly body. A healthful climate builds a healthy body. The climate of the Earth has been divided into three Zones: Frigid, Temperate, and Tropical.

Zone of Death

1. The Frigid is the Zone of Death. Its intense cold and perpetual snow make living there impossible.

Many brave explorers in times past have frozen to death in attempts to discover the North Pole.

Zone of Hibernation

2. The Temperate is the Zone of Partial Death. It is the Zone of Winter Sleep or Hibernation, a state of semi-death, in which the vital functions of animals and plants fall to the lowest ebb possible without death resulting.

The vegetables and animals naturally at home in that zone are so peculiarly constituted by Nature that they have ability to go into a deep sleep in winter. The animals not so constituted are clad in heavy coats of warm fur. When man first attempted to live in the Temperate Zone, he was forced to clothe his body with the hides of these fur-clad animals that he murdered, in violation of the Law of God. This was the birth of the clothing industry. It arose from transgression of Gods law and has developed into an economic burden that does its part to crush man.

Humanity in the Zone of Hibernation pays billions annually to clothing mongers for clothes for protection from the killing cold. This economic burden is unknown to the natives of the tropics, and man brought it upon himself by his attempt to live where it isn't made to live.

Zone of Life

3. The Tropical is the Zone of Eternal Life. It is the zone of eternal summer. It furnishes food perpetually, spontaneously produced by Nature. It is filled with evergreen

vegetation, giant animals, and giant people. The men of some tropical races are all over seven feet tall (Ripley).

A deep secret of Nature is concealed in the fact that no part of the Adamite period is so strongly painted as the Warm Climate. Manta dwelling naked in the Edenic Garden (Genesis 2:25) proves there is no alternative of summer and winter, but one warm season of eternal growth.

Suggested Reading

THE GREAT LAW by Professor Hilton Hotema — 42 Marvelous Lessons — The greatest work ever produced in the field of health and life. It tears away the veil between the two phases of Life: Physical and Spiritual. It teaches that the highway to health, happiness, success, and long life lies in knowing yourself, your construction, constitution, and powers. (1963) approximately 270 illustrated pages.

LIVE 1400 YEARS - Creation - *The Empyreal Sea* (How High Do You Climb?) The title was changed several times by Professor Hotema.

THE MAGIC TEMPLE - by Professor Hilton Hotema. This is the body in which you dwell during your days upon the earth. This is the greatest work on the human body that the world has ever seen or had and is just as magic as the work Magicaliam. Medicine is as big a fraud as religion, and the medical trust kills outstanding opponents who expose it. The whole story is told in this amazing book which gives truth others are afraid to tell.

HOW I LIVED TO BE NINETY (1966) by Prof. Hotema. Offset, Illustrated, many photos of Prof. Hotema.

All available from: www.frontlinebookpublishing.com

The Ancient Secret
By Dr. G. R. Clements

The evidence shows that ancient science knew the secrets of prolong youth and longevity. These ancient men knew how to preserve the body's vitality and prolong its days. They lived in harmony with this knowledge before the Flood and, at the age of 150, were still youngsters just beginning to have children. Jared was 162 and Lamech was 182 when they begat their first child, and Noah was 500 when he begat his first child (Genesis 5:20, 25, 28, 32).

Ancient records show that ancient people knew secrets of Nature unknown to modern science or modern doctors. They knew how to (1) promote health, (2) preserve youth, and (3) prolong life.

But a group of men interested only in money and not in the betterment of humanity are not going to kill the goose that lays the golden egg by learning how to promote health, then teach that knowledge to the people. For a world of health would mean the end of doctors and all lines of commercialism that live and thrive on the miseries of man.

The ancient formula of Perpetual Youth was known to the ancients, and they lived nearly a thousand years. But that knowledge apparently was lost with the death of Noah, as evidenced by the fact that after his death the life-span rapidly declines.

Adam lived 930 years (Genesis 5:5), and Noah lived 950 years (Genesis 9:29). From Adam to Noah the life-span averaged 912 years. From Shem, son of Noah, to Nahor, only eight generations, the lifespan averaged 354 years; Shem lived 602 years and Nahor 148.

Shem's life-span was 348 years shorter than his father's. That was the first appreciable decline from the days of Adam. In eight generations after Noah the lifespan had decreased to 148 years — a startling decline of 802 years in eight generations.

What was the ancient secret that seems to have been lost with the death of Noah?

Conquer Death

The world's history is composed of the issues of Life and Death. The Ancient Masters said: --

Death is swallowed up in victory (1 Corinthians 15:54). There shall be no more death, neither sorrow, nor crying, neither shall there be any more pain; for the former things are passed away (Revelations 21:4). Perpetual Youth and Eternal Life have been the dream of philosophers from the dawn of humanity. Down thru the centuries man has searched for the Fountain of Youth and Elixir of Life. Prophets and poets in every age have told of a time when the pain of disease would be unknown and the sting of death unfelt.

For what is more precious than Life? What is a man profited if he gains the whole world and loses his own life? — Matthew 16:26. Death is the drop of gall in the cup of pleasure. Childhood fears it. Old age dreads it. Even disease, poverty, crime, shrink from release by it. The beast loves life no less than man. Consequently, how to promote health, preserve youth, and prolong life was the first subject to engage man's serious attention. It is still the leading thought.

The First Scientists

Recent discoveries teach us to have greater respect for Ancient Science. It was the growth of countless ages and was apparently born in India (Genesis 11:2). The sacred writings of the Hindus give their ancient history an astounding chronology converging thousands of years (Peerless Atlas, 1903, p. 149).

Modern science is in its infancy. Its career has hardly begun, and its progress is impeded by its materialistic views. It rejects the doctrine of the Supreme Power and a Life Principle, It holds that Life is what it does. Life is "the expression of a series of chemical changes," says Osler, the greatest doctor America ever produced. This leaves the Living World without a law and leaves science laboring in the dark. Recently discovered records show the Ancient Masters knew secrets of Nature unknown to us. The fact they lived for centuries is evidence they knew how to preserve the body and prolong its youth. Adam was 130 when he begat his first child and lived 930 years. Methuselah was 187 when he begat his first child and lived 969 years (Genesis 5:3, 5, 25, 27).

This vital knowledge seems to have been lost with the death of Noah. He was the last of the Ancient Scientists who appears to have known the secret of the ages. For then, after his death, the decline in the life-span was very rapid. As time passed, the decline continued at an alarming rate. In eight generations after Noah, it had dropped from 950 to 148 years — an astounding decline of 802 years! Behold man's tremendous loss: See his most precious treasure slipping from him, In only eight generations approximately 85 percent of his life was lost.

Experience teaches that when man saw his life leaving him so fast, his heart was filled with horror. He was being hurried to the grave while yet young in years; and demon death was striking him down ere his work had hardly begun.

The very picture makes one shiver. With the grim monster standing at his door, slaying many while in the flower of youth, with failure meeting every effort to find ways and means to defeat the demon, the race in desperation turned at last to the idea of a Life Beyond the Grave as the best that could be done. That was the abject surrender. For man is not the victor until he has discovered the Law that makes him master of his destiny and gives him power to control the conditions that destroy him.

Universal Law

Modern science fails in its work because it rejects the doctrine of a (1) Supreme Power, (2) Life Principle, and (3) Universal Law. On that point Dr. Walter writes: --

"Everything in accordance with law is the testimony of both Science and Revelation; and man becomes the possessor of Earth's treasures as soon as he has discovered the laws of their production. The first real step towards exact knowledge is the discovery of the law. All the investigations, speculations, the inductions that man can invent or employ, are worthless until the work is completed by this discovery" (*Vital Science,* p. 205).

Modern science has incessantly searched for the Fountain of Youth but has failed in its work because it has not been scientific in its search. All searchings lead in circles until the fundamental fact is discovered that Man is part of a World of Law and Order. The Supreme Power and Life Principle are facts of existence, and the Law of Life is as certain as the Law of Gravitation. But medical schools refuse to recognize these things and continue to grope in darkness.

Every event that takes place occurs under the control of one law, sustained by one force. In spite of the fact the medical world denies it, this Principle of Nature applies as forcibly to the human body as to the rising sun. "No symptom of health or disease, no pain or pleasure, weakness or strength," writes the shrewd Dr. Walter, "is ever found in a living organism except under the control and direction of the one law, sustained by the one power — the law that solves all physiological problems" (*Vital Science*, p. 22).

That statement of Law shows the absurdity of hunting for health in magic waters and mysterious brews, poisonous drugs, and filthy serums. It shows that health is not a question of doctors and dope, of vaccines and poisons. It shows why the "practice of medicine" must always be what it has always been — the practice of nonsense and so declared by leading doctors of the world.

Prof. Majendie, the celebrated French physician, said:

"Medicine is a great humbug. I know it is called science, Science indeed: It is nothing like science" (Densmore, p. 209).

Dr. Ernest Schwenninger, the famous physician to Prince Bismark, wrote:

"Doctors call medicine 'recognized science.' It is recognized ignorance" (Densmore, p. 207).

What little we know of the operation of the Law of Cause and Effect teaches that, barring accidents, the Health and Duration of the Living Body depend upon the conditions supplied. Dr. Walter states:

"If we supply the conditions for health, health will follow with unerring certainty; but if the conditions are for disease, disease will sooner or later follow as the Law of Adjustment will permit." (V.S., p. 122).

That statement agrees with the views of the Ancient Master who said:

"Whatsoever a man soweth, that shall he also reap" (Galatians 6:7).

It is science and law that we cannot sow the seeds of disease and harvest a crop of health. Nor can we force into the body such poisons as medicines, drugs, vaccines, and serums and be favored with good health and long life. Let us carry the principle farther: If we supply the conditions of prolonged youth, then with unerring certainty we shall have prolonged youth. Also, if we supply the conditions of long life, then, barring accidents, long life will follow with unerring certainty.

This appears as the basic principle of the knowledge lost with the death of Noah. Let us proceed with certainty in a straight-forward manner through infinite time into infinite results.

Our next step is to learn how to apply our new discovery of an old secret. There is no use to turn to modern medical lore, for the bungling work of medical men shows they are wandering in darkness. Their schools teach that health comes from forcing destructive poisons into the body. Centuries of experience proves this is wrong. We must look for a better source. We turn to the teaching of the Ancient Masters, who worshipped Truth instead of Mammon.

Chapter 9
Path to the Glorious Life

Ages of experience show without exception that Simplicity, Frugality, and Self-Denial (Matthew 16:24) are the basic qualities that constitute the Path to the Glorious Life.

Listen to the words of Socrates, the sage of centuries ago:

"Know thyself. Earthly goods advance not their possessor. To want nothing is divine. To want the least possible brings one nearer to divine perfection" (Encyc. Americana, 1938, vol. 25, p. 220).

"The less physical Man becomes through the conquest of his Desire, the less he needs. The less Man needs, the nearer he becomes like gods, who use nothing and are immortal."

"The Wise Men of the East (Matthew 2:1) considered Desire a "foul monster," to be conquered by Self Mastery. In the "Message of the Master" we read:

"As the flame is dinned by the smoke; and the bright metal by the rust, so is the Understanding of Man obscured by this foe called Desire, which rageth like a fire and is difficult of being extinguished.

"Thy first task is to conquer this foul dweller in the Mind. Mastering first the Senses and Sense Organs, do thou then proceed to put to death this thing of evil.

"The Senses are great, and powerful. But greater and more powerful than the Senses is the Mind; and greater than the Mind is the Will; and greater than the Will is the Real Self.

"So, thus recognizing the Real Self as higher than all, proceed thou to govern the Personal (Physical) Self to conquer this foul monster, Desire, most difficult to seize, and yet possible of mastery by the Real Self; then bind him fast forevermore, thy slave instead of thy master" (p. 44).

Body-Building Material

The Living Body must be furnished constantly with suitable Building Material. This material consists of (1) Air, (2) Water, and (3) Food.

Before the advent of gas, the engine, the deadly exhaust of which has poisoned the air of civilization; and — Before commercialized health boards began polluting the water of civilization with poisonous chemicals, under the pretense of purifying it — Food was the only element of body-building material to which it was necessary to give particular consideration.

Due to the fact that Excessive Eating is the rule of every animal when food is plentiful, the function of eating is a matter in which the Mind must incessantly exert itself in order to hold Desire in Subjection. While both Air and Water come before and are superior to Food as body-building material, it is not possible to injure the body by the free use of these, provided they are pure and fit for consumption. The same is not true of Food, unless it is strictly natural and consists of juicy fruits, such as grapes, oranges, mangoes, peaches, plums, melons, and the water of coconuts.

These are the natural food of man; and aside from these, one must be careful not to eat to excess. For the surplus above the body's needs, not being used, decomposes and ferments in the body and poisons it. Sylvester Graham (1794-1851) often said that a drunkard may reach old age, but a glutton, never. The truth of this assertion is proven by experience. Drakenberg, a Dane, buried in the cathedral in Aarhus, Denmark, lived 346 years — "And reached this advance age in spite of the fact that he was more often drunk than sober." writes Dr. Arnold Lorand in his *Old Age Deferred*, p. 18.

Frugal Eating

Contrary to medical theory that man should eat freely of what doctors call "good nourishing food," for health and long life, the opposite of this theory is proven in practice to be the Path to the Glorious Life. A leading case in order is that of Ludovico Cornaro, described in the Ency. Americana as a 'Venetian nobleman" (vol. 7, 1938, p. 707). The account states:

"From the 25th to the 40th year of his age, he was afflicted with a disordered stomach, gout, and slow fever, till at length he gave up the use of medicine and accustomed himself to extreme frugality in his diet. * * * In his work upon the *'Birth and Death of Man,'* composed a few years before his death, he says of himself:

"I am now as healthy as any person of 25 years of age. I write six or seven hours; and the rest of the time I occupy in walking, conversing, and occasionally in attending concerts. I am happy, * * * my imagination is lively, my memory tenacious, my judgment good, and what is most remarkable in a person of my advanced age, my voice is strong and harmonious.'" -- Ibid.

Of Cornaro, Dr. J. E. Cummins writes:

"Cornaro (was) the greatest modern food scientist,. He was born an invalid and became a drunkard. At the age of 40 he was a physical and mental wreck, and his physicians told him repeatedly that he could not live.

"Cornaro began to experiment with foods. He found he could live best on 12 ounces of solid and 16 ounces of unfermented wine daily. With the exception of 12 days, he lived on this ration for over 63 years. Within one year he had recovered his health. His wife adopted the same course and bore children late in life. Both lived beyond the century mark. On his 78th birthday, Cornaro's friends begged him to increase his ration a little. Reluctantly he agreed to a 14-ounce allowance. In 12 days he was stricken with fever and violent pains in his right side. He at once returned to the 12-ounce ration but suffered for 35 days. This was his only illness in a period of 63 years, Life became more beautiful the older he grew. He wrote several books, his last after the age of 95. He died at the age of 103" (Dietetics).

Cummins holds that man would have better health and longer life if he ate only one-fourth of what he usually consumes, He says:

"In India, at the present time, people eat but one meal a days and that in the evening. Occasionally they have a little rice water to drink in the morning. They know nothing of digestive troubles.

"In Bible times people ate but one meal a day, and biblical law required that the laborer be paid daily so he could buy his meal. The ancient Persians lived on one meal a day. The Greeks and Romans lived on one or two meals a day. No nation has quite equaled the Greeks in physical perfection" (Dietetics).

K. L. Coe, writing in Correct Eating and Strength, March, 1931, refers to people who live healthy and long and to the natives of India in particular. He observes:

"Numerous instances of longevity are reported from various quarters, proving that man, under certain circumstances, can live to a much greater age than is customary.

"Perhaps the most striking of these in recent times is furnished by Dr. Robert McCarrison, of the Army Medical Service in India, who reports that in a colony in the Himalayan region he found natives who were so old that it would be hard to believe their records correct, yet he was not able to detect any error in their way of keeping these records. Ages well beyond 250 years were common. He found men of well attested age up to 150 years recently married and raising families of children.

"Men said to be well over 200 years of age were working in the fields with younger men and doing as much work and looking so much like the younger men that he was not able to distinguish the old from the young. These people were restricted by religious dogma to the products of the soil for food, no animal products being permitted except a small amount of milk or cheese, which were considered luxuries.

"He reported these people were never sick. They had none of the usual diseases of civilized countries, as they could not afford the expense of the habits which cause these diseases. "During his nine years in that region, there were no cases of indigestion, constipation, appendicitis, etc. In fact, no sickness of any sort. He might as well not have been there, except for the illness and surgery within the army post itself. It is possible these people live so long and are so free from disease because they live almost entirely on natural foods."

What a lesson civilized man could learn from the simple habits of the people of India and other tropical regions of the earth. But he considers himself so far above these people that he looks down upon them with disdain. It has been shown by experiments that great danger lies in excessive eating and in eating artificial and prepared foods.

Dr. Charles W. De Lacy Evans, M.R.C.S.E., etc., surgeon to St. Savior's Hospital, England, and author of several scientific works of unusual interest, wrote an admirable book entitled *"How to Prolong Life."* In the chapter on "Instances of Longevity in Man and in the Animals and Vegetable Kingdoms," he reviewed nearly 2,000 cases of persons who lived more than a century. After discussing all their various habits and customs, he says:

"We find one great cause that accounts for the majority of cases of longevity — moderation in the quantity of food" (Densmore, p. 295).

Again Dr. Evans writes:

"Among instances of longevity, we have the ancient Britons, whom Plutarch states 'only began to grow old at 210 years." * * * Their food consisted almost exclusively of acorns, berries, and water" (Ibid).

In the February 7, 1878 issue of the Lancet, lot, a London Medical journal, was reported the case of Miguel Solis, of San Salvador, a half-blood Indian, who was then living at the age of 180. The account stated:

"Dr. Hernandez found this man working in his garden. He attributed his long life to his careful habits and eating only once a day. He had been accustomed to fast on the 1st and 15th of every month. He chose the most nourishing foods and took all things cold." (Densmore, p. 297).

Dr. Arnold Lorand warns against heavy eating. He observes:

"It is certain that more people die from eating too much than too little. It is surprising to consider how little food man can exist upon for a long time and remain in good health; and it is certain that the foundations of many diseases are laid by excessive eating " (*Old Age Deferred,* p. 280).

Value of Fasting

It is a rule without exception that all animals eat to excess when food is plentiful. Little does modern man know of the damage done to his body by excessive eating. In case of the lower animals, experimental tests show the effect of fasting and excessive eating. On this point Prof. C. M. Child, Chicago University, writes:

In case of the lower animals, experimental tests show the effect of fasting and excessive eating. On this point Prof. C. M. Child, Chicago University, writes:

"Experimental investigations, carried through a number of years in the Department of Zoology of the University of Chicago, have shown these flatworms, when well fed, grow old just as the higher animals do, but that they may be made young again in various ways.

"When these animals are deprived of food, they do not die of starvation in a few days. * * * They are able to live for months upon their own tissues. During the time of fasting they become smaller and may be reduced to a minute fraction of their original size. When fed again after such fasting, they show all the physiological characteristics of young animals. With continued feeding, they go again through the process of growth and of becoming old and may be made young again by fasting.

"One group of the worms was well fed, and every three or four months passed through the cycle of growing old and reproducing. * * * The other group was given just enough food to maintain the animals at a constant size. The worms of this group remained alive and in good physiological condition without becoming appreciably older as long as the experiment continued — that is, during some three years. With abundant food, this species may pass through its whole life history — in three or four weeks. But when growth is prevented by fasting, it may continue active and young for at least three years, as the foregoing experimental has demonstrated and doubtless for a much longer period. According to the observation of Julian Huxley, the extension of the life-span in this experiment is roughly equivalent in man to keeping a person alive from the time of Chaucer (1340-1400) down to the present date."

Fasting and frugal diet kept worms alive for three years that die in three or four weeks when well fed. Had the experiment continued longer, the worms perhaps could have been kept alive longer.

If this could be done with a man who lives 100 years, he would live 4,000 years. And science regards as fiction the Bible story that Adam lived 930 years.

Bernard MacFadden of Physical Culture Fame believes that fasting will do for man, in a measure, what it does for worms. He writes:

"I have consistently maintained* * * that the body can be revived and made more youthful in every way, mentally, physically, etc., by fasting. It is my firm belief that we can live for an almost unlimited period, maybe for centuries, if the youth-building possibilities of a prolonged fasting process, followed by the use of nourishing elements that would fortify vitality, are properly investigated and understood in all their details." — Physical Culture Magazine, Aug. 1925.

A few years ago, Prof. Huxley, son of the elder Prof. Huxley, performed an experiment on young earth worms. He fed a family as they usually eat, except one worm, which he isolated and fed the same way, but now and then he made it fast. It was alternately fed and fasted.

The isolated worm was still alive and vigorous after 19 generations of its relatives had been born, lived their regular time, and died. Huxley explained the matter by stating that heavy eating clogs the life channels and hastens death.

Applying this procedure to man with similar results, instead of his dying at 100 and his friends thinking he had lived long, he would live almost 2,000 years. And science regards as fabulous the Biblican account that Methuselah lived 969 years.

Shall we believe God bestowed more power on worms than on man, the crowning-work of Creation and Lord of the living world? That seems illogical. In this instance, if a man who dies at 50 could extend his lifespan 19 times, as in the case of the worm, he would live 950 years, the exact age of Noah (Genesis 9:29).

Is this coincidental, or does it reveal a secret of Nature known to the Ancient Masters? Did they understand the rejuvenating effect of a (1) controlled diet with (2) alternate fasting? We shall see.

Chapter 10
Fountain of Youth

Following this cue, Dr. H. M. Shelton says, "The Fountain of Youth is within you" (Orthobionomics, p. 291). Modern science has searched for it in all parts of the world, but never within the Body. The Ancient Masters knew that within the body there actually flows a River of Living Water (John 7:38). Ancient Science knew this thousands of years ago (Genesis 9:4). But modern science knew it not until 1618 A.D., then refused to believe it when told.

In 1618 the famous Dr. Harvey proclaimed his discovery of the circulation of the blood — and the medical schools only scoffed and sneered. Hume, the historian, states:

"No physician in Europe who had reached the age of 40 ever to the end of his life adopted Harvey's doctrine of the circulation of the blood" (Wilder, *History of Medicine*, p. 204).

With the death of Noah the knowledge of the circulation of the blood seems to have been lost, and ages later the ancient Greeks believed the arteries were air tubes because they found them empty in the dead body, and they were named "artere" from "air."

This belief continued until the time of Harvey, who discovered the arteries did not carry air, as taught by medical schools, but were tubes filled with blood during life and empty only after death had fully drained their contents into the veins.

The doctors were content to ridicule Harvey at first; but when they began to realize they were not able to disprove his statement, they were filled with rage and organized a system of persecution against him, until it is said they broke his heart (Dr. Wm. H. Hay).

Blinded by false theories unto this day, medical schools cannot see the Fountain of Youth when it stares them in the face. Their work shows they search not for Truth and consider nothing that fails to support their preconceived belief, founded on a false premise. They hide their ignorance in the darkness of a dead language, and the multitude is mesmerized by that which it cannot understand. The Ancient Masters not only knew of the circulation of the blood, but asserted that "the life of all flesh is the blood the re-of" (Genesis 9:4). At another time they wrote:

"The life of the flesh is in the blood. It (blood) is the life of all flesh. The blood of it is for the life thereof. For the life of all flesh is in the blood thereof" (Leviticus 17:11, 14).

Behold the striking repetition of the Basic Principle of Nature in order to make a lasting impression of a fundamental fact.

Law of Disease and Cure

The Vital Fluid is the River of Living Water, the Fountain of Youth. It turns the Wheels of Life and is the Healer and Rejuvenator of the flesh. It is composed of what man breathes, drinks,
and eats. By these functions he replenishes the River of Living Water, which gives him control of the condition of the Vital Stream. The Fountain of Youth is what he makes it; and from the magic power of its silent chemistry there issues forth either health or disease, depending on man's living h abits, Man reaps just as he sows (Galatians 6:7).

This basic knowledge the Ancient Masters possessed for ages and used it effectively to cure disease, rejuvenate the body, and prolong life. By their work they proved their wisdom. They taught that —

1.   *Disease results from stagnated circulation and vitiated blood.*

2.   *Purification of the blood and acceleration of its circulation is scientific cure.*

3.   *The means to accomplish this are supplied only by the body.*

4.   *The body makes blood and purifies it. Nothing else can do this vital work. The wisest chemist cannot make one drop of blood.*

5.   *The supply determines the method of procedure.*

6.   *The procedure must be natural to be favorable.*

7.   *Being natural, results are positive and permanent.*

This is the Ancient Law of Disease and Cure. It made an exact science of the ancient art of healing. Details of this law were concealed from the multitude. The law was never known to the doctors of Europe and is not known now to the medical schools of this country.

During the Dark Ages of Europe (450 to 1550 A.D.), when the people there sank almost to the Stone Age in ignorance, and even kings could neither read nor write, and that land was swept with epidemics which the doctors could not handle. The doctors can do but little better now. The "flu-epidemic" of 1918 swept this country with disease and death and swept the doctors off their feet. They were helpless and admitted it. Experience shows that the object of medical schools is to perpetuate a certain system of thought and nothing more. They know but little now about the body's functions; and previous to the modern discovery of the circulation of its fluids, they knew much less. Until Harvey made that discovery, the modern world was without a fundamental principle upon which to base any attempt to rejuvenate the body. This knowledge is still so new that medical schools are in darkness on the subject of rejuvenation.

It is now known the blood is a vast transportation system with many functions. It carries new material to all parts of the body to repair and renew its constantly decaying cells and carries off for elimination their waste and excretory products. This recently discovered knowledge proves the River of Living Water is the Fountain of Youth, by which every part of the body, every hour of its life, is incessantly repaired, renewed, rejuvenated, from the softest cell to the hardest bone. That is Regeneration in every sense of the word.

This newly discovered knowledge the medical schools know not how to use; and the puzzled doctors are asking, "why does the body grow old and die? Why don't it go on forever?"

The great Metchnikoff was jeered by his medical brethren when he answered these questions. He declared that deterioration of bodily structure and old age are due to minute quantities of poisonous substances in the blood. His work furnished the first logical explanation in modern times of the degenerative changes that occur in the body and why. His findings have been confirmed by research workers, including Dr. George W. Crile, Dr. James Empringham, and Dr. Alexis Carrel.

1.   Crile says: "*There is no natural death. All deaths from so-called natural causes are merely the end-point of progressive acid saturation.*"

2.   Empringham says: "*All creatures automatically poison themselves. Not Time, but these toxic products (in the blood) produce the senile changes we call old age.*"

3.   Carrell, famous biologist of the Rockefeller Institute, asserts: "*The cell is immortal. It is merely the fluid in which it floats that degenerates. Renew this fluid at proper intervals, and give the cell nourishment upon which to feed, and, so far as we know, the pulsation of life may go on forever. Quickly, involuntarily, the thought comes: Why not*

with man? Why not purge the body of the worn-out fluids,
develop a similar technique for renewing them — and so win
immortality?"

How simple: That process suggested by Carrel was
followed by the Ancient Masters. They knew the River of Living
Water is the Fountain of Youth, the purpose of which is to
sustain the body and maintain its integrity. But every power that
builds also destroys upon a reversal of the lever. And so the body
receives its death-blow from the blood due to man's evil work.

The blood is replenished, renewed, several times each day.
But with what? Here is the root of the problem: The Fountain of
Youth is renewed with foul air, impure water, decaying food,
intoxicants, soda fountain slops, tea; coffee, chocolate, tobacco-
juice, nicotine and all that filthy substance of civilization which
enters the lungs and stomach--and in time man dies of "a
progressive acid saturation. A startling discovery Regeneration is
a scientific fact: The discovery is so new that its possibilities
have not even begun to be realized.

Old age and early death are due to poisons in the blood,
says Metchnikoff — and his stupid medical brethren jeered.
Purge the blood of its poisons and it becomes the Fountain of
Youth in essence. The Ancient Masters knew whereof they
spoke when they said:

"Thy youth shall be renewed like the eaglets (Psalms
103:5).

Medical schools have never investigated the body's
Regenerative Processes. But Naturologists are making strides in
that direction. H. Carrington describes the matter as follows:

"The moment the last morsel of food is digested and the
stomach is emptied, a reconstruction process begins — a new
tissue formation, owing to the fact that the broken-down cells are
being replaced by (new) healthy ones: which is Nature's way of

repairing any destroyed or injured part of the body. This replacement of cells means replacement of tissue; replacement of tissue means a new stomach has been constructed — a stomach NEW in every sense of the word, as new in every anatomical sense as is the filling in of wounds or between the fractured ends of bones" (*Vitality, Fasting & Nutrition*, p. 490).

Now we know why man sinks so rapidly into decay and death. Medical schools don't know it, but the custom of eating three to six and seven times a day gives the burdened stomach no chance to empty itself and repair its worn and wasted cells.

It is not strange that civilization is cursed with stomach and bowel complaints, with indigestion and constipation. How do doctors treat these ailments? They give the poor patients poison called medicine and feed them more food. We shall come to this again.

Land of Centenarians

According to statistics, little Bulgaria, in southeastern Europe on the Black Sea, is the land of Centenarians in the civilized world. The Encyc. Americana says:

"The climate (of Bulgaria) is healthy, and the country enjoys the reputation of possessing more centenarians than any other in Europe. People said to be 105 to 125 years of age are not uncommon, * * * Over 70 percent of the people are engaged in agriculture* * * Fruits and vegetables are raised in abundance, * * * Wine is plentiful and cheap." — vol. 5, 1938, p.1

In 1927 a commission of Bulgarian doctors visited a large number of these old people and reported they lived on a frugal fare of fruits, vegetables, and milk products, usually sour milk and butter-milk; that they are lean to the point of being underweight, according to medical standards. Only one of the group was found to weigh as much as 168 pounds, the majority weighing between 122 to 130 pounds. They are industrious. Their habit is early to bed and early to rise and to sleep uncovered as much as possible. Almost all of them are farmers and live in the open air and sunshine.

Every investigation reveals the dangers of high living and excessive eating. While Bulgaria has 58 centenarians per 100,000 of population, in the United States, the land of abundance and gluttony, of intemperance and debauchery, of doctors and drugs, of vaccines and serums, we can boast of but four centenarians per 100,000 of population, with the number steadily declining.

There is no mystery surrounding the conditions of vigorous health and long life. Narrow is the way, and few there be that find it (Mathew. 7: 14). Simplicity, Frugality, and Self-Denial are the sign-posts pointing to the Path of the Glorious Life (1 Corinthians 9:25).

Dietetic Ignorance of Doctors

The multitude looks to the doctors, and the doctors admit they don't know.

Many conscientious persons lead a righteous life in all things but eating. They go wrong in eating and in the choice of foods because they follow the foolish advice of the doctors.

Experience shows that doctors know practically nothing about food and feeding, and some frankly admit it. The rest might as well, for their work discloses their ignorance.

These things are well known and have often been published by leaders in the health field. Dr. K. Bain of the U. S. Children's Bureau is reported in the press of October 24, 1941 as addressing the American Dietetic Association in session in St. Louis-and telling the group that —

"A stumbling block in medical education is the weak nutrition training of doctors and nurses."

Why this "stumbling block"? because medical schools have consistently refused to recognize the fact that there is any relation between diet and disease. For how can food be the cause of disease when the medical world holds that disease is the work of germs? And how can disease be cured except by the use of poisons and serums to kill the "germs"?

It was the dietitians, not the doctors, who carried on their work in the face of bitter medical ridicule, which brought to light the startling discovery that it is not Proteins, Fats, and Carbohydrates which play the important part of nutrition, as taught by the medical world, but the elusive, little-known and less understood elements now called Vitamins and Mineral Salts.

The doctors and the controlled press worked hard to laugh and ridicule this discovery into oblivion. But the consistent results obtained by dietitians in feeding certain food to the sick were so amazing that the multitude has grown food-conscious in spite of the cries of quackery and fraud by the doctors. The marvelous experiments with the worms show the dangers of being what the doctors call "well-fed." If you are well-fed, you are on your way to early decrepitude and early death. When the worms were well-fed, they grew fast. No doctor would condemn that for that is the condition for which the doctors are striving. Feed children freely to make them grow fat and fast. Behold the results. See how little the doctors know. The well-fed worms grew fast; they reached maturity fast; they began to decline fast; and they died fast.

But no orthodox doctor would attribute food and fast growth as the underlying cause of early decay and early death in man.

Law of Analogy

Man is not a worm. No. But his body is subject to the same law. Therefore, a worm has some analogy to or with a man. The analogy is legitimate and natural. It is valuable as pointing out the Path to the Glorious Life. Scholars have recognized the value of analogy. Prof. W. Stanley Jevons, University College, London, writes:

"The whole value of science consists in the power which it confers upon us of applying to one object knowledge acquired from like objects, and it is only so far as we can discover and register resemblances that we can turn our observations to account. * * *

"Whoever wished to acquire a deep acquaintance with Nature must observe there are analogies which connect whole branches of science in a parallel manner and enables us to infer of one class of phenomena what we know of another. It has happened on several occasions that the discovery of an unsuspected analogy between two branches of knowledge has been the starting-point for a rapid course of discovery" (*Principles of Science,* 6, 631).

There is no branch of Science from which difficulties have not been removed by the certainties of a kindred branch, when analogically compared with it, or which, on similar comparisons, does not furnish new hints and valuable illustrations.

The result of the experiment with the worms constrains us to turn to the Biblical account of the early patriarchs. They did not develop fast; they did not grow old fast; they did not die fast.

Adam was 130 when he begat his first child, and he lived 930 years (Genesis 5:3, 5). Methuselah was 187 when he begat his first child, and he lived 969 years (Genesis 5:25, 27).

Then comes a startling change. Noah lived 950 years, but his grandson Arphaxed who begat his first child at the early age of 35, lived only 438 years (Genesis 11:12, 13). Peleg, great grandson of Arphaxed, begat his first child at 30 and died at the age of 239 (Genesis 11:18, 19). Nahor, only eight generations after Noah, begat his first child at the age of 29 and lived only 148 years (Gen. 11:24, 25).

Man now grows faster; he reaches maturity faster; and he dies faster. Behold this law of Nature. Here lies a great secret. Science has never tried to fathom it because Science regards the stories in Genesis as fiction. It is fair to infer from Biblical statements that in the time of Adam and Noah it required 100 years for man to reach maturity, and he lived nearly 1000 years. John Gardner, M.D., *of England, in his book on Longevity, writes:*

"Before the Flood, men are said to have lived 500 and even 900 years. As a physiologist, I can assert positively there is no fact reached by science to contradict or render this improbable. It is more difficult, on scientific grounds, to explain why man dies at all than to believe in the duration of human life for a thousand years."

The Great Change

Dr. Walter says that under the same conditions the same result is obtained; and under a change of conditions, it is evident there must be a corresponding change of results. As we review the lives of the patriarchs thru the ten generations from Adam to Noah inclusive, and the eight generations after Noah, a remarkable change appears in the length of the life-span.

The life-span from Adam to Noah inclusive averaged 912 years, and Noah died at the age of 950. There now comes a change. The life-span from Noah1s son Shem to Nahor, inclusive, averaged only 345 years. Shen lived 602 years, and Nahor died at the early age of 148.

The life-span of Shem was 348 years shorter than Noah's, his father (Genesis 11:11). That was the first appreciable decrease from the days of Adam; and there was a reason for it.

While the medical world holds that such things just happen, law and logic do not support that view. Under the same conditions the same result is obtained. That is the law.

Passing to Nahor, only eight generations after Noah, the life-span decreased to the short period of 148 years (Genesis 11:25). An amazing decline of 802 years in a few generations, as previously stated. We saw what happened to the worms when well-fed. We saw the rejuvenating effect of the (1) controlled diet combined with (2) alternating fasting.

Is this the formula of Perpetual Youth that Noah took with him when he passed into the Great Beyond? Have we discovered the reason why the life-span declined so fast after his time?

Being Well Fed

The experiment with the worms undoubtedly reveals, in part at least, the changed conditions that caused the changed results in the life-span of the ancient patriarchs. There must have been a change in food and feeding. Men must have been well fed; and they grew fat and fast, as do the foolish people of the U.S. The experiment with the worms shows the result of being well-fed and of growing fat and fast. It reveals the secret why the Ancient Masters so consistently taught the virtues of Simplicity, Frugality, and Self-Denial.

Ages of experience is showing that a man created to himself new wants and a plentiful food supply, his health declined and his life-span decreased. We find that —

1. The dawn of Man pictures him in a friendly climate, where he is naked and not uncomfortable, satisfying his

*hunger with the delicious fruits of vines and trees growing in
a garden that he was ordered to dress and to keep* (Genesis
2:7, 25).

Then, in addition to these fruits, he turns to herbs and
vegetables, which he obtained from a more avaricious earth,
as the reward of his work.

2.   *He next domesticates wild beasts and drinks as milk the
excrements of their blood. This is the beginning of the
beastly development in man. For Like begets Like.*

Lastly, he slays the dumb brutes and feasts on their festering
flesh. This is the beginning of hybridism in man. For *"Man is,
what he eats,"* declares Dr. W. H. Manwaring, Professor of
bacteriology and pathology, Stanford University, California.

Chapter 11
Physiological Rest

We know the value of rest. Fasting means Rest for the vital organs. The Ancient Scientists knew the value of resting the vital organs. Modern science may make that discovery someday. But it will not happen so long as modern science continues to believe in the theory that Life and Energy come from Food. Fasting and frugal eating is the Path to the Glorious Life.

Frugal eating nourishes the body without overworking the internal organs. Fasting gives these organs needed rest. We saw what this means in case of the worms. The body of man is subject to the same law. The ancient master recognized Fasting as the Great Remedial Measure and resorted to it in instances of illness. The measure was also employed generally to improve human health; and the rulers, by official edict, proclaimed periodic fasts throughout their realm (2 Chronicles 2:03). The Bible states:

"The word of the Lord of hosts came unto me saying: The Fast of the fourth month, and the fast of the fifth, and the fast of the sixth, and the fast of the seventh, and the fast of the tenth, shall be to the house of Judah joy and gladness" (Zechariah 8-19).

Fasting twice in the week was a common custom in the days of Jesus (Luke 18:12). The disciples of John fasted often (Luke 5:33). David fasted (2 Samuels 12:16), and so did Ahab (1 Kings 21:27). Moses fasted forty days (Exodus 34:28). Elijah fasted forty days (1 Kings 19:8). Jesus fasted forty days (Matthew 4:2). These wise men knew how to promote health and prolong life. They knew that doctors and drugs possess no magic nor healing power.

Science of Rejuvenation

Modern man knows nothing about Rejuvenation. Modern science knows so little about it that it cannot discuss the subject intelligently. Much evidence appears in the writings of the Ancient Masters to show they thoroughly understood the matter.

Until Harvey discovered the circulation of the blood, the Process of Rejuvenation was unknown to modern science; and it was considered the height of ignorance for one to suggest the possibility of Rejuvenation. Previous to Harvey's discovery, medical schools knew so little about the body's functions that they had no fundamental principle upon which to base an attempt to prolong human life. Out of Harvey's discovery came that knowledge which has led to some progress in this field. But the body's functions are still so little understood that doctors are not qualified to conduct properly the Process of Rejuvenation. As a result of this incompetency —

"Not even one day has been added to the span of human life," says the great scientist Carrel, who adds:

"A man of 45 has no more chance of dying at the age of 80 now than in the last century. ... "

"Science follows on plan. ... Men of science know not where they are going. ... We shall have to go farther and build up a real science of man. ... The science of man is still too rudimentary to be useful" (*Man The Unknown,* pp. 23, 142, 178, 179).

Here is a medical leader declaring the medical world knows next to nothing about Man.

This profound ignorance of the doctors is proven by the fact that the best of them die at early ages. Before us lies the daily paper of Nov. 20, 1941, with the account that Dr. Richard C. Foster, president of the University of Alabama, "died tonight of creeping paralysis," at the age of 46. With few doctors living to reach the century mark, with most of them dying in their early years, it should be expected of them to sneer the Biblical statement that the Ancient Masters lived 900 years. Before Harvey's discovery, medical schools knew not that Vital Force, under the Law of Change, is constantly engaged in tearing down the old and worn tissues and rebuilding them again of new material supplied by the "river of life" How can such a machine wear out? Impossible.

It has been only within the last 50 or 60 years that medical schools knew that all cells, tissues, and organs of the body are always renewed by the Fountain of Youth and always ready to perform their allotted work. When the discovery was made that the River of Life is actually the Fountain of Youth within the body, the doctors, in astonishment, quickly inquired: Why does the body grow old and die? To find the answer, feverish research has been done, and this is the reply:

1. *"There is no physical reason at the present day why man should die"* (Dr. Wm. A. Hammond, late Surgeon, U.S. Army).

2. *"With a perfectly balanced in-doctrine system, man would live forever. In fact, your Fountain of Youth is within yourself"* (Dr. Friedenburg, noted Physician of New York).

3. *"The human frame as a machine is perfect. It contains within itself no marks by which we can possible predict its decay. It is apparently intended to go on forever"* (Dr. Munroe).

The Ancient Masters knew how to make the River of Life the Fountain of Youth. But they kept the secret concealed from the multitude and have been careful to leave no complete outline of it.

A few advanced physiologists, losing faith in the "practice of medicine" and looking in other fields for the Elixir of Life, have at last discovered that secret by piecing together their findings and comparing them with ancient writings.

Their first discovery was so simple it amazed them. They found that all animals, when ill refuse to eat. Here is a law of Nature, said they. The teaching of medical schools is diametrically opposed to it. They insist on feeding patients "plenty of good, nourishing food to keep up their strength."

Strength comes from food, says the medical schools, and stupid man so believes. But strength comes not to the invalid, no matter how well fed; while the brawny athlete gains in strength as he prepares for his performance on one scanty meal a day and reduces his weight considerably.

The physiologists did more thinking. They observed the (1) high death-rate under regular medical procedure of feeding patients well, and they grew more skeptical.

They studied (2) the cases of animals that invariably fast when ill and almost always recovered health. This law of Nature works, said they. Then they studied (3) the writings of the Ancient Masters and found frequent references to fasting. The Ancient Masters knew the law.

Lastly they noticed the Ancient Masters never (4) filled their stomach with food when preparing for unusual events. They always fasted. They not only knew the law, but obeyed it,

With this valuable evidence to guide them, they began to experiment on worms, with results so favorable that they turned to man. Always were the same good results obtained.

By fasting their patients, the recoveries were so remarkable as to be amazing. In their enthusiasm they called it the "Wonder Cure." It was tried by Dr. Adolph Mayer, an eminent German physician, and he wrote:

"I assert that fasting is the most efficient means for correcting disease" (Fast Cure — Wonder Cure). Dr. Moeller, superintendent of the Closchwitz sanitarium, said:

"Fasting is the only natural evolutionary method whereby, through a systematic cleansing, the body can restore itself by degrees to physiological normality."

As disease is degeneration, reasoned the physiologists, a procedure that consistently cures disease and restores the body's normal physiology must be a Process of Regeneration. And they are right. That is how leading physiologists stumbled onto the Law of Regeneration.

The Bible shows that when preparing for extraordinary events the Ancient Masters always fasted. They knew by experience that fasting improved their physical and quickened their mental powers.

The case of the worms and the findings of modern physiologists prove they were right. Their work shows they were not pseudo scientists, as we have today, but true scientists of the first water.

Delving deeper into the subject, these physiologists found that constant and heavy eating is the path to disease and premature death. That explains the high death rate of doctors, who practice what they are taught and die early as a result.

The custom of eating from three to six and seven times a day sends man into disease, degeneration, and early death. The body becomes burdened with more material than it can use. The surplus creates a dangerous condition. It stagnates the "river of life," damages the delicate machinery, clogs the life-channels, and saturates the whole system with deadly toxins.

1.   What did Dr. Empringham say? *"All creatures automatically poison themselves."*

2.   What did Dr. Crile say? *"All deaths are merely the endpoint of a progressive acid saturation."*
3.   What did the great scientist Metchnikoff say? *"Deterioration of bodily structures and old age are due to poisonous substances in the blood."* And his dumb medical brethren jeered.

Physiologists show that man, by his living habits, makes his blood the (1) sparkling river of life, or the (2) stagnant stream of death. Investigation shows that as waste and toxins accumulate in the blood, the delicate cells become flooded with filth and choked and poisoned by their own excrement which the over-worked organism is unable to eliminate.

Many of the cells decay and die. All of them are more or less damaged. The person becomes ill. He is frightened. He thinks he is going to die and calls a doctor. What does the doctor know? Ask Metchnikoff. They jeered him when he explained the cause of disease, decay, and old age.

That is disease. That is how disease is built. That is why the body sinks into degeneration and early death. That is the Ancient Secret. That is the broad highway modern man travels in ignorance, as he follows his blind leaders, the dumb doctors who jeered the great Metchnikoff when he explained the cause of decay and old age.

Ask yourself this question: Can disease be cured by giving patients medicine and more food? God forbid. Do you wonder why patients so treated so often fail to recover? Do you see why patients so treated die while yet in the flower of youth? Medical ignorance of the body functions is the answer.

Upton Sinclair knew something of the virtues of Fasting. He wrote:

"The great thing about the Fast is that it sets you a new standard of health."

In spite of the fact that man follows faulty courses of living in most respects, and seldom concords with the law of his being, the constant renewal of the cells by the "river of life" holds old age at bay for a considerable period of time. That is the reason why some men live for a century in spite of bad habits and without knowing a thing about the Law of Life or the body's processes.

> *1.   Fasting rejuvenates because it permits the "river of life" to flow freely, thus allowing the renewal processes to exceed those of disintegration.*
> *2.   Fasting enables the depurative organs to purge the "river of life" of toxins and the body of diseased, worn out, and low-grade tissues.*
> *3.   Fasting permits the body to clean house, purify its fluids, normalize its chemistry, and regain its proper equilibrium. That is Regeneration.*

The rejuvenation effects of Fasting was known to the Ancient Masters. It is positive and certain and so evident as to be readily observed. The effects are visible in the external parts of the body and in the function of the sensory organs. Sight, smell, hearing, taste, and touch all show marked Improvement. The sense of smell, for instance, improves so much the faster is often nauseated by foul odors that are usually unnoticed by him.

Prof. Sergius Morgulis, Nebraska College of Medicinelwrote a masterly work entitled *"Fasting & Undernutrition,"* in which he relates specific instances of Rejuvenescence through Fasting. He states:

"The acuity of the senses" is increased by fasting and "at the end of his 31 days" abstinence from food, Professor Lavanzin could see twice as far as he could at the beginning of the fast. There is more proof. Under the process of fasting, wrinkles, pimples, and blotches disappear; and the skin regains its youthful appearance. The same regenerative effect takes place in all organs and glands. Dr. H. M. Shelton says:

"The fasting body begins to grow small; and, in order to maintain the integrity of its vital organs, it utilizes all the surplus material it has on hand. Growths, deposits, effusions, dropsical swellings, infiltrations, fat, etc., are absorbed and used to support these organs.

"With no digestive drugery on hand, Nature employs the long desired opportunity for general house cleaning purposes. Accumulations of surplus tissues are overhauled and analyzed; and the available component parts are turned over to the department of nutrition, while the refuse is thoroughly and permanently removed" (*Regeneration of Life,* p. 93).

Under the rejuvenative effect of Fasting, the River of Life is purged of its poisons and becomes the Fountain of Youth. Abnormal growths and dropsical swellings disappear, running sores heal, enlarged glands return to normal size, and the vital organs grow stronger, including weak hearts. H. Carrington writes:

"The fact that hitherto weak hearts are strengthened and cured by fasting proves conclusively that any such unusual symptoms, observed during this period, denotes a beneficial reparative process" (*Vitality, Fasting & Nutrition* p. 464)

Physiologists show that nerve energy, during a fast, is conserved and transmitted in more powerful waves to the vital organs, enabling them to improve in force and function and to eliminate more fully the waste and toxins which accumulate under constant feeding.

"The degree of rejuvenescence" in such cases, says Professor Child, "is in general proportionate to the degree of re-organization in the process of reconstruction of the piece into a whole."

It is obvious that the degree of regeneration will not be so great in a decrepit man of 60 or 70 as in the case of that man at the age of 45 or 50. Now for an amazing example in the case of man: Doctors Carlson and Kunde, University of Chicago, showed that a fast of 15 days temporarily restores the tissues of man of 40 to the physiological condition (age) of those of a youth of 17.

Astounding! Not only does Fasting stop the onward march of physiological age for man like it does for worms, but it even turns back the hands of measuring time for him like it does for worms.

We have found the Key of The Ancient Secret of regeneration, known to the Ancient Masters but concealed from the multitude (Mark 4:11). They spoke often of cases of rejuvenation, but their writings have not been understood. Now we can read their words with better understanding.

His flesh shall be fresh as a child's; he shall return to the days of his youth (Job 33:25). And thy youth shall be renewed like the eagle (Psalm 103:5). *These things worketh God oftentimes with man* (Job. 33:29).

Modern science has branded these biblical statements as fables and fiction. But advanced physiologists are proving the statements are true. Fasting made the flesh of a man of 40 as fresh as that of a child's, and his youth was renewed like the eagle's. That is exactly what the Ancient Masters wrote. But in our ignorance we could not understand and refused to believe. To remain ignorant is to remain a slave (Wayland). Ignorance is the power that keeps man in darkness.

Under the process of fasting, a man of 40 regains 23 years of life. This means that a man of 64 in solar years would be only 41 in physiological years. That explains why we, at the age of 66, feel in body and mind as we did in 1919. On this test of Rejuvenation, we base our belief that we still have 60 or 70 or even more years to live, barring accidents. One of our uncles recently died at 93, and he knew nothing about the Law of Life. Our lifetime study of the subject should enable us to outlive him 30 or 40 years.

In this respect we are encouraged by the fact that it is harder to bring back the condition of youth when lost than to keep from losing it. We keep it by living in harmony with the law. We have done that for forty years and are as active and supple now as we were forty years ago.

An article in the press of Feb. 27, 1938, stated that Tapsi Bishan Das Udasi, of India, was reported to be 172 years old but "appears to be not over 40." He claims to know the secret of rejuvenation but will tell no one. The press of June 11, 1933, related the death of Li Ching-yun at the amazing age of 256. He was born in 1677 and had papers to show that he was congratulated by the Chinese Government on his 150th and 200th birthdays. Sir William Temple states that the Brahmins of India, who live mostly on fruit and green herbs and drink only water, live to be 300 years old.

An item in the press of 1923 stated that Sadhu Swami, of Karinganji India, was living then at the age of 330. Peter Maffins, in his history of India, tells of Numisde Oogua who died in 1566 at the age of 370. His teeth, beard, and hair were renewed four times — the work of regeneration.

Biologists assert that if the cells of a man of 40 can be regenerated to equal those of a youth of 17, it is possible to keep them indefinitely in that condition. If that is possible, then it is certain within the limits of the possibility (V.S., p. 204).

By exhaustive experiments, Dr. Morgulis proved beyond the shadow of a reasonable doubt that Fasting is a dependable process of regeneration and the only one known to man. He found that during a fast the body does not tear down its tissues nor impair them structurally. The cells are merely reduced in size, as in the case of the worms. They decrease in bulk but not in number.

Strange to say, the nuclei of the cells lose so little bulk under a fast that they become relatively larger in ration to the rest of the cell, as in the case of children. And, as in the case of children, such cells have the same capacity for assimilation and growth which characterizes the cells of the young. This is further evidence that fasting rejuvenates and accounts for the fast growth of tissue as feeding begins after fasting ends.

After the fast has purged the blood of toxins and the body of clogging waste and decaying the diseased cells, healthy cells are built of better material to replace those cast out of the body during the fast. That is Regeneration. That is the secret of the Ancient Masters. Know the law, and observe it. That is the way to keep your body active and vigorous.

In the days of Adam and Noah, man ate only the juice of fruits of Nature and drank the water of coconuts. They ate less in a day, perhaps, then than modern man eats in one meal. The duration of their youth extended over several centuries (Genesis 5:32), and they lived most a thousand years.

Chapter 12
Lost Health Regained

Many persons have sunk almost to the brink of the grave, as Cornaro did, and then turned to Nature after losing faith in doctors and their worthless methods and not only regained health, but lived a long and useful life. There is the case of John Banes, of England, who suffered in middle life from a severe illness of a chronic nature and was unable to find any doctor who could help him. The doctors then told him he could not get well and had only a short time to live. He turned to Nature, adopted a strict mode of living, and lived to be 128 years old,

Capt. Goddard E. Diamond, of San Francisco, at the age of 79 was suffering from a severe case of hardened tissues and blood vessels, with stiffness of the joints. Yet for 30 years he had lived a life of what is called Vegetarianism. The tissues of his legs and back were so hardened that he could not rise from a chair nor sit down without extreme discomfort, and he often required the aid of an assistant. The tissues of his arms and hands were so stiff that it was with difficulty that he held a knife and fork to feed himself. The doctors being unable to give him relief, he turned to Nature, adopted a strict mode of living, and was still alive in 1915, at the age of 119, being born in 1796, while George Washington was still living and had seen 29 presidents of the U.S.A. elected. When Diamond was over 100 he was doing gymnastic work with an athletic club that few young men could equal. At the age of 100 he rode a bicycle and walked 20 miles a day. He attended social events, and when he was 110 he once danced most of the night with anathletic girl of 16. The cases of this kind come before us, and we are prone to ponder the question of how long man could live, if he began to live properly from the start and kept it up to the end.

It is a fact that a body once weakened by disease will always remain below par. The scientist Carrel says, "We bear forever the scar of those events" (*Mans The Unknown,* p. 170).

While a diseased heart, liver, kidney, pancreas, stomach, etc., may be regenerated to such extent that it fails to bother its owner, and may give good service for years, such organ cannot again become normal. That fact is proven by the evidence that a wound, though it heals, yet leaves a scar composed of low-grade tissue.

A fatty heart, a fibrous liver, a diseased mucous membrane — these cannot return to their normal state. But as the original size of an external scar diminishes with the passage of time, so the diseased organs, by a process of strict living, will continue to improve with the passing of years.

Process of Sclerosis

Sclerosis means hardening and thickening of cells and tissues. This is the condition of decrepitude. It is due, in a large part, to deposits in blood vessels, glands, tissues, and cells. The deposits accumulate until a state of hardening occurs, and this is old age.

The symptoms of aging appear in ratio with the progress of hardening. If the body of a boy were stiffened in the same degree as that of a man of 80, the boy's body would show similar signs of age. If it is possible to prevent hardening, it is possible to prolong youth and postpone old age. This can be done. The Ancient Scientists knew the secret.

Capt. Diamond's case supplies valuable data. After 30 years of vegetarianism, he is afflicted with general sclerosis. His diet, no doubt, consisted chiefly of cereals and cereal products. There contain large quantities of minerals that stiffen joints, tissues, and blood vessels, "and as a class," writes Densmore, "are the worst adapted as food for man."

Bread, "man's so-called 'staff of life,' is to a great extent the cause of premature death," continues Densmore (p. 290), who adds: "Dr. Rowbotham, of England, adduced profound proof in his work published 50 years ago that cereal foods tend to the ossification (hardening) of joints and tissues and to produce decrepitude and early death" (*Natural Food of Man,* p. 290).

Densmore adds that the same conclusions have been reached independently by leading doctors of England, France, and Germany. Dr. C. C. Hibbs, in an article on Dental Decay, says:

"The grains are responsible for nearly all of man's disease, for wheat, oats, rye, and barley are no more a part of man's food than oranges the food of a cow, or grass the food of cats. ...

"Eliminate grains from the diet, and decay in children's teeth will cease. Tarter and pyorrhea will disappear. The hospitals will fold up, and medicine will be a dream. All the doctors on earth with their 'vast' medical experience cannot disprove this statement.

"The medical profession dare not take a group of children and feed them according to Nature's law for six months then truly publish the results" (*You Can't Eat That*).

Cereals and cereal products constitute the basis of modern man's food. Knight, in his "Food of Man," states that early man could not have known of cereals, pulses, and starchy vegetables; that the cereals have been developed from grass plants now unknown to Botanists; and that tropical regions, the natural home of man, are filled with the luxuriance of Nature's provision for man in the way of luscious fruits (Densmore, p. 393).

The case of Capt. Diamond shows the process of sclerosis can be halted not only, but its evil effects largely removed by proper living. A person affected with sclerosis should begin the rejuvenation process with a fast, drinking only water, live in the sunshine and Pure air, take all the exercise he can with comfort, and a sweat bath every day.

Cases of Fasting

Most people never fasted and are afraid to try it. Medical doctors, groping in the dark, foolishly assert it is dangerous to go six or seven days without food. Nothing better could be expected of a group of misguided persons who believe that building health is the same as the process of fattening hogs. In thousands of fasts, ranging from thirty to 100 days, no deaths have been known to occur that could be attributed to the fast. The press of January 14, 1937, states that Dr. S. H. Tanner; Minneapolis physician, abstained from food for 40 days in 1880 to settle an argument with a colleague of the New York Neurological Society.

For 18 days Tanner took neither food nor water. Then he began drinking from 40 to 70 ounces of water every 24 hours. When the fast ended, Tanner had lost 35 pounds but suffered no ill effects. His pulse and temperature remained almost normal throughout the fast.

The press of May 2, 1937, reported that Jackson Whitlow, a religious zealot, fasted 35 days. His wife stated that he refused food "on the Lords orders." His weight dropped to 92 pounds, but he suffered no ill effects. The press of August 13, 1938, stated that Mrs. Mae Zimmerman fasted 63 days to gain relief from the pains of arthritis. She lost 38 pounds.

Mary Mitchell, age 27, Santa Ana Calif., a practical nurse, in January, 1927, broke a fast of 64 days. She weighed 202 pounds when the fast began and 158 when it ended. For the first five weeks of the fast, she continued her work as nurse; and during the remainder of the fast, she worked about her home, preparing food for members of the family and said this did not tempt her to eat. Her health and energy were much improved by the fast.

In June, 1926, George H. Johnson walked from Chicago to Bald Knob, Pa., without food, covering the 578 miles in 20 days in a contest to win a prize. He said he was in fine condition when the journey ended. Maybell Collins of South Africa fasted 101 days in 1931 to reduce according to the press. She weighed 232 pounds when the fast began and 169 when it ended. She said she was in good health, went out to parties, and carried on with her public singing.

An English businessman, age 53, who refused to permit the use of his name, began a fast October 30, 1932, under the case of John W. Armstrong, who has conducted hundreds of fasts. He took nothing but water until 6:30 p.m. Feb. 7, 1933, a fast of 109 days. He could have continued 10 days more had it been necessary. His weight dropped from 191 to 132 pounds. He said he was on his "last legs"; that nothing did him any good. He tried fasting as a last resort and regained health. C. H. Cowan fasted for 42 days. When he began he weighed 165 pounds, and when the fast ended he weighed 135 pounds (Dewey, p. 118)

Milton Rathburn fasted 35 days. When he began he weighed 211 pounds, and when the fast ended he weighed 168. He said: °I feel like a boy again. I think I could vault over a six-foot fence" (Dewey, p. 126). Miss Estella Kuenzel, age 22, lost her mental health to a degree that death became the final object of desire. A fast of 45 days restored her health (Dewey, p. 140).

Leonard Thress, age 57, recovered his health by fasting 50 days His weight dropped from 209 pounds to 133. He declared that all his ailments left and he never felt better (Dewey, p. 149).

Elizabeth Westing, music teacher in poor health, fasted 40 days. Her weight dropped from 110 pounds to 93. On the last day of her fast, she was able to sing with unusual clearness and power and ended her fast without losing a day from her duties as a teacher of music (Dewey, p. 155).

Dr. Edward H. Dewey, from whose work *"The Fasting Cure"* we have excerpted the last five cases above, considers excessive eating such a curse that he writes:

"The ways of the kitchen and dining room are the ways of disease and death, ways whose ends are prisons, asylums, scaffolds, to a far larger extent than is dreamed of by the fathers and mothers of the land" (p. 182).

In the press of January 25, 1938 was an account to the effect that for 10 years Giovanni Succi travelled thru Europe giving exhibitions, severely controlled, extended for periods of 30 to 40 days, during which time he was in the public eye day and night. Included were 80 periods of 30 days fasting and 20 periods of 40 days of fasting — a total of 3200 days of rigorous fasting.

There are 3650 days in 10 years of 365 days per year. As Succi fasted 3200 days in the 10 years, he fasted eight years and 280 days.

Eternal Life

We hear much talk, in these days of deceptive propaganda, about what medical art has done to improve man's health and increase his life-span.

The great scientist Alex Carrel, M.D., in his book, *Man The Unknown,* 1935, makes this statement:

"We (medical doctors) have not succeeded in increasing the duration of our (man's) existence. A man of 45 has no more chance of dying at the age of 80 now than in the last century.

"This failure of hygiene and medicine is a strange fact. In spite of the progress achieved in the heating, ventilation, and lighting of houses, of dietary hygiene, bathrooms, and sports, of periodical medical examination, and increasing number of medical specialists, not even one day has been added to the span of human life" (p. 178).

That sums up the empty result of 3,000 years of medical work. What profit has it brought man? Yet it has cost civilization billions upon billions of dollars.

Many E. Forbers wrote a book, copyright 1926, printed in Paris, France, in which she makes surprising statements that meet the test of law and logic. From this book we excerpt the following:

Prof. Monit, of Harvard, in his book, Age, Growth, and Decay, says:

"Death is not a universal accompaniment of life. In many of the lower organisms, death does not occur so far as we know at present, as a natural necessary result of life. Death with them is purely the result of accident, some external cause. Our existing science leads us to the conclusion, therefore; that death has been acquired during the progress of evolution of living organisms."

So we find science supporting the Garden of Eden story, which tells in allegorical form that something man did evolved disease and death.

Ancient Scientists possessed the secret of longevity and perpetual youth. They lived in accordance with this knowledge before the Flood and at 150 were still young, just beginning to have children. Methuselah was 187 when he begat his first son, and Noah was 500 when he had his first child (Genesis 5:20, 25, 28, 32).

Thomas Parr died at the age of 153. Dr. Harvey, modern discoverer of the circulation of the blood, performed an autopsy and found his organic condition good. No signs of decay appeared in his organs or glands. His death was attributed to over-eating of rich food at the royal household of the King, who had invited him thither, as he wanted to learn from the most interesting of his subjects the secret of long life.

As the fierce, flesh-eating races front the West overwhelmed the peaceful fruitarians of the Far East, the secret how to preserve vitality and prolong life was concealed from the invaders and for centuries afterwards was confined to a small group, handed down from generation to generation.

Function of Life

The function of Life is to create, sustain, and inhabit. Creation carried with it the power to sustain, and that which is sustained by Life should be immortal.

Life develops man to maturity. After that, the body should show no change to a downward trend. Life is eternal. But it can be forced to withdraw from the form it has organized. When this occurs, the form disintegrates. But this withdrawal is not necessary nor inevitable.

If the function of Life is to create and develop man, to carry him on to maturity and sustain him, it should not begin at that point to impair and destroy the body it has made. Life would not be consistent with its purpose if it deliberately and willfully destroyed that which it had created.

Having developed man from a speck, there is no reason known why life should not maintain him for an indefinite period. Leading physiologists assert it would do so, if he obeyed the law. The end is hastened by the habit of trying to doctor and cure the Effects of transgression, instead of removing the Cause. In other words, the belief in the doctors is another factor that leads to early death.

Maud Levett writes:

"There will be no dust to return to dust when a better brain and a better knowledge of the properties of food and air will do away with the separation of man from his body."

Death is not natural. (If it were, it would not have been necessary for God to pass the death sentence on man — Genesis 2:17). Death does not inhere in living forms. There are organized forms of minerals, vegetables, and animals that never die.

Death comes to all creatures that violate the law, or have not the intelligence and capacity to control and regulate their conduct and environment. These qualities man has, thus making him superior to all other animals. Man may rise superior to his Environment by reason of his great intelligence. He is competent to discover and abide in a favorable Environment and thus supply conditions that would make him immortal. The Bible says that man shall conquer Death (1 Corinthians 15:55).

That idea is beginning to take hold of thinking men. With the capacity for Intelligence that would make man a god, the small amount of intelligence developed is used to obstruct the operation of Lifers function.

The body is subject to a law that takes no account of time. The same process that makes the body old and withered would, upon a change of conditions, make it young and keep it vigorous.

In the vegetable and animal world, the arrival at maturity, flowering, fruiting, and decaying is a universal process which no one will deny. But to hold this process applies with equal force to man is to deny his higher plane of existence and to see no difference between him, the master of himself and his environment, and the beasts, which are ruled by appetite and passion and are unable to command anything. Man's body is subject to the law of matter, along with the birds and beasts. But he has a brain which, if developed, enables him to rise superior to the animal plane and to supply conditions that transform degeneration into regeneration. (This ends the excerpts from the book of Mary E. Forbes.)

The Chemical Basis

"The particular chemical composition of the body," writes Mary E. Forbes, "calls for food of like chemical composition." She says the medical world knows nothing about this fact. The faulty work of doctors proves she is right. In *"The Science of Life,"* Wells and Huxley discuss Old Age under the heading: "The Wearing Out of the Machine." They say in part:

"The chemical basis of this wearing out is at present not understood. Old Age seems to be associated in some way with defective calcium metabolism. The brittleness of senescent bones is due to the reabsorption of lime salts into the blood. Moreover, there seems to be an accumulation of poisonous substances in the blood. *** Sooner or later one or the other of the essential organs fails and the body dies. It is important to realize that our cells do not die because mortality is inherent in their internal structure. They die because they are parts of a very complicated system based on cooperation, and sooner or later one of the tissues lets the others down.

"As a matter of fact, living matter is potentially immortal. If one keeps a culture from the tissues of a young animal and takes subcultures regularly, the race of cells can apparently go on growing and dividing indefinitely. Death is a consequence of incomplete organization. The tissues die because they are parts of an imperfectly balanced body," asserts Wells and Huxley. Be it so, but the imperfect balance is the fault of man, not of the body.

The (1) Power to establish and the (2) Mechanism to maintain a perfect balance in all departments of the body is inherent in the organism and requires no aid from doctors or nurses. The body needs only to be permitted to operate unhampered in order to preserve its equilibrium. The process of repair and renewal is automatic in operation; and science has shown that it is capable of continuing indefinitely, unless hindered by man's faulty habits.

Experience shows that man's mode of living has become so faulty and so foreign to the Law of Life that he begins to decline almost as soon as he attains maturity, and often before; and he sinks down in death when he should be in his prime.

Summary

1.   The findings of science support the parable of the Garden of Eden, showing that what man does to himself is the Cause of disease and death (Genesis 2:17).

2.   The evidence shows the ancient patriarchs knew how to live to preserve the body and prolong its youthfulness. Methuselah was 187 when he begat his first child, and he lived 969 years (Genesis 5:25, 26).

3.   There can be no deterioration in the body (a) sustained by Eternal Life and (b) maintained in perfect balance and repair by the River of Life.

4.   The chemical composition of the body demands material of the same chemical composition from the River of Life. Such material is natural, unheated, uncooked, and unseasoned foods, as produced by Nature and pure air.

5. Medical schools are ignorant of this law and recommend substances detrimental to the body, resulting in changes in the body's chemistry, which produce imperfect balance, decay, and death.

6. Modern science says, "The chemical basis of this wearing out (of the body) is not understood." The Ancient Masters possessed this knowledge and used it to preserve youth and prolong life.

7. Science shows that living matter is potentially immortal and subject to a law that takes no account of Time. The cells die not because mortality inheres in them, but because of chemical changes and accumulations of poisons, which produce an imperfectly balanced body.

8. Death is the sequel of faulty organization, arising from the faulty work of man, done usually in ignorance and due to lack of knowledge of the Law of Life.

9. These secrets the Ancient Masters knew and taught in the schools of the Ancient Sacred Mysteries, of which Jesus was an initiate.

10. Simplicity, Frugality, and Self-Denial are the primary qualities that constitute the Path of the Glorious Life.

11. The less physical Man becomes thru the conquest of his Passions and Desires, the less he needs. The less Man needs, the more he can become like gods, who use nothing and are immortal,

He that over-cometh shall inherit all things (Revelation 21:7). *Few men there be in civilization who have the Will Power to overcome the twin demons, Passion and Desire* (Matthew 7:14).

Chapter 13
The Holy Bible

Most of us are taught in our youth to regard the Bible as a sacred book — that is, a book containing an authoritative revelation from God on the history, duty, and destiny of man.

We are taught to accept peculiar and unreasonable stories in the Bible as true because they are in the Bible. We grow up, taking for granted that Moses, Aaron, Abraham, Isaac, and Jacob were real persons. That the history of the Jews is faithfully reported in the Old Testament; that the prophets wrote the books attributed to them; that Jesus Christ was born at Bethlehem on the first Christmas Day over nineteen hundred fifty years ago and crucified on the first Good Friday about thirty-three years later; that the Apostles and Evangelists wrote the books which bear their names; and that such is the reason why there is a Bible and a Christian Church today.

The advance of natural science, and especially of cosmogony, geology, anthropology, and biology, finally exploded any authority attached to the Bible on the subjects of the origin of the earth and the creation of man. These subjects are scientifically discussed by Professor Hotema in his great work *Cosmic Creation,* in which it is shown that our universe was evolved from a cloud of incandescent gas of enormous proportions, such as giant telescopes show are scattered by the thousands throughout endless space and, according to science, the earth was at first a ball of white-hot substance when it formed in and from that cloud of gas; and it required thirty million years for it to cool to its present temperature.

In cosmogony, geology, anthropology, biology, and other natural sciences, researches have discovered and classified a vast mass of facts, none of which support any existing religion, but all of which must be the basis of any religion which can be adopted as a correct and factual way of life by modern, rational, logical people. It is preposterous to expect such people to "believe" in biblical data that are contrary to common sense, knowledge, and experience. The absurdity of this is attested by the decline in church membership in recent times and the growth of Free Thought.

Reasonable, intelligent men and women will not surrender their common sense and knowledge in the name of an unscientific religious system. To them, religion must be logically acceptable, not emotionally desirable. In referring to the Bible, M. M. Mangasarian wrote: "A book which claims infallibility, which aspires to absolute authority over mind and body, which demands unconditional surrender to all its pretensions under penalty of eternal damnation is an extraordinary book and should, therefore, be subjected to extraordinary tests." (*The Neglected Book,* p. 5).

He calls the Bible the Great Paper Idol of the Churches, asserts that "all idols are veiled," and shrewdly adds: "The Veil is the Idol. Uncovered, they scare nobody."

It is our purpose in this work to uncover this Great Paper Idol of the Church. By reasonable discussion, logical argument, and scientific facts we shall lift the Veil and let the Light of Knowledge shine on this Great Paper Idol invented by the priesthood.

Bibliolatry

Bibliolatry is blind, superstitious worship of the Bible based not on a knowledge thereof, but on the fraudulent claim of the church that every word in the book is a direct revelation of its God. Most of those who exalt the Bible above all other books have not studied it — usually haven't even read more than a chapter here and a passage there. No other book is more reverenced and less known than this so-called "Book of Holy Writ."

Ignorance of the Bible is indispensable to faith in the Bible. Also, it is this ignorant veneration that makes it dangerous for anyone to reveal the facts behind the Bible's compilation.

Once upon a time, when the Church possessed greater power, anyone who studied the Bible or questioned its "holy authenticity" was either hacked to pieces or burned to death. Even now, challengers are persecuted as much as public opinion and the law will allow.

In 1926 M. M. Mangasarian wrote (*The Neglected Book,* p. 14): "It is a matter of history that in the name of this Jewish-Christian volume, which people do not read and are but superficially acquainted with, nearly a hundred million lives in Europe alone have been destroyed."

Before the 19th Century, if one attempted to investigate the background of the Bible and state his findings, his life was in danger. With the beginning of the 19th Century, the vast power which the Church had ruthlessly wielded for a thousand years declined to where it was safer for one to question the contents of the Bible. The result has been that an enormous amount of amazing light has been thrown on the Bible by unprejudiced researchers.

Until the 19th Century, the hieroglyphics of Egypt and the cuneiform inscriptions of Babylonia and Assyria were undecipherable and not understood, and the Bible was our sole authority for the history of man prior to the rise of Greek civilization. However, with the discoveries by archaeologists of the key to the hieroglyphics and cuneiform inscriptions was revealed the surprising existence of highly developed civilizations long before the time previously assigned, on the authority of the biblical genealogists, to the creation of man.

Also, the Egyptian and Assyrian monuments enabled the history of the ancient civilizations, during the period to which the Bible relates, to be reconstructed with a great degree of accuracy. While there are points of agreement between the biblical record and the ancient monuments, there are many important points where the messages cut in stone not only fail to confirm the biblical records, but flatly contradict them.

And so, the Bible as "The Word of God" shows that God got mixed up in His work, relating what He did not do and erroneously describing what He did do.

Heathenish Superstition

What was the religion of Europe, Egypt, and Asia Minor before the Roman Catholic Church was founded by Constantine in 325 A.D.? Heathenish Superstition or Paganism we are told in the histories and encyclopedias prepared for us by the Church. From what literature did the Church Fathers compile their Bible? From the scrolls of those Superstitious Heathens.

Why was Chrysostom so happy when he boasted in the early part of the 5th century that —

"Every trace of the old philosophy and literature of the ancient world has vanished from the face of the earth"— Bible Myths, Doane.

History states that after the birth of Christianity and the compilation of the Bible, the Church engaged in a systematic and ruthless campaign of destruction of the "old philosophy and literature" of the Heathens. The great Alexandrian Library, comprising 700,000 volumes of the Superstitious Heathens, was "stormed and burned in 391 A.D. by a mob of fanatic Christians, led by Archbishop Theophilus" (Ency. Americana). Why? To conceal the fact that the literature of the Heathens did not tell the same story the biblical makers put in their Bible. And why does the Church still get so excited when some of that ancient literature is discovered? Because it fears the facts may be found. The facts have been found, and they are startling. They are related in books by many able authors, and these books are burned by "fanatic Christians," or else they are converted after reading the books and become Atheists and Communists.

Among other things, these facts show there is no early history of the Hebrews, as related in the Bible. And their reputed ancestors, Abraham, Isaac, and Jacob, are not historical figures, but mythical heroes, analogous to those of Homer and Hesiod. Originally, these mythical heroes appear as gods associated with the local sanctuaries in Palestine and were taken over by the Hebrews when they settled in that land.

The Pentateuchal narratives, the long discourses between God and the mythical Moses, and many other events, are fabulous compilations of the crafty priesthood for a religious purpose, prepared centuries after the Hebrews occupied Palestine, and are absolutely worthless as history.

Professor Hotema states in his great work Land of Light that the Bible is basically a book compiled from ancient poetry, drama, and fables and falsely presented by the Church as a record of Ancient History and of Revelation direct from its God.

Birth of Jesus

A history of the Bible is a history of Christianity, and a history of Christianity is a history of the Church. The Church claims that Christianity is based on the Bible. But there is no Bible until Christianity is born; and there is no religious system of that name until the Church is born.

The Bible and Christianity are unknown in history until the Church was born in 325 A.D., in the Council of Bishops of

Nicea, a city of Bithynia, in Asia Minor on the south side of the Black Sea.

The Council was convened by Constantine, who purposely picked a place remote from Rome so the Romans would be in the dark as to what was occurring.

The proceedings were worse than a political convention in the USA. It was a knock-down and drag-out affair. No quarters were asked, none were given, and no compromises were in order. Constantine had his scheme formulated, and it had to be approved — or else. Briefly, his scheme was a blending of all the religious systems of his Empire, to end the strife among the various sects and make his Empire safer, and to unite them under one god, to be born by the union of the two leading gods of the realm.

This unition was the point that precipitated the bitter battle. Neither side wanted to give up its god. The debate was furious and wrathful, and when the proposition was put to a vote, the no's vastly outvoted the ayes. Then Constantine went into action. The bishops were not going to run his realm. So he summoned the Roman Guard, standing by for any emergency, and had the recalcitrant bishops removed from the convention. And that was the last of them.

Then the proposition was put to another vote, and Constantine's scheme carried unanimously. And that is the long-hidden secret as to the miraculous birth of the only begotten Son of God (John 3:16). He was born in a convention of bishops by the union of Hesus Kristos, two solar symbols, and became the god of the spurious religion. The Church was now established; its god was born; the wealth of the mighty Roman Empire supported the scheme — and the multitude could like it or lump it. When the startling story reached Rome, it created a sensation. And when Constantine returned, his reception was far from enthusiastic.

He met the situation by sending an army of workers some seven hundred miles east of Rome, to the site of the old city of Byzantium, and there they built him a new capitol, named for its founder — Constantinople. He made the city thoroughly Christian, built churches in every Quarter, and eradicated all traces of "Heathenish Paganism" (*Story of The Church,* by John C. Monsma).

Chapter 14
The Nicean Council

J. M. Roberts was an American lawyer, born in 1821 and died in 1888. He wrote a book titled *Antiquity Unveiled,* published in 1894 after his death. It soon became a rare volume and hard to get because it was burned by Christians as fast as they could find it.

This work tells that Jesus Christ of the Bible was born in the Nicean Council in 325 A.D. by a union of Hesus Kristos. From that work we excerpt amazing information as follows:

The data of the proceedings of the Nicean Council came from Eunomius, one of the bishops who was thrown out of the convention for opposing Constantine's scheme.

An account of this man appears in Smith's Greek and Roman Biographical Dictionary, in which it is said that all his writings were destroyed by imperial edict. Even so were destroyed the writings of the Christians who attempted to answer his charges. Eunomius disclosed that the real issue of the heated controversy of the Council was the unition of the two gods.

His disclosures reveal the reason why no record was published of the proceedings of the most important Christian Council. The absence of such a record has ever been a puzzle to modern Christian authors and critics. That a record was made is certain, but for damaging reasons that could not be avoided, it was never published. All that has been permitted to come down to us as to the objects and actions of that Council have been collated by the learned and pious Dr. Nathaniel Lardner.

Prior to the 4th century, there was frequent and general mention of Kristos and his worship to the east of Rome. But nowhere can be found any authentical mention of Jesus Christ.

For it was not until after the Nicean Council that the name Jesus Christ was ever given to this god.

And why was the name Jesus linked with Kristos from that time forward? To appease the worshippers of Hesus. When Eusebius wrote his Ecclesiastical History after the Nicean Council, he admitted the name Christian was then hardly known at all. He said:

"The name Christian is indeed new and has not long obtained over the world" (Ant. Un. p. 638).

Here is the unqualified admission by one of the originators of what is called Christianity, that Christianity, as such, was new as late as 325 years after the alleged birth of Jesus Christ. That system was merely adopted and promulgated in the name of Jesus Christ by Eusebius and his Christian coadjutors after the Nicean Council. This evidence shows that Jesus Christ of the New Testament is just a combination of the names of the Sun Gods Hesus and Kristos. It was a master stroke of governmental policy on the part of Constantine to seek to blend the prevailing religions of his day into one system that would reconcile the warring interests of the various priesthoods who kept the Roman people in a constant state of turmoil and contention.

Pious Fraud

Widely scattered through hundreds of ancient and modern volumes, most of what we shall say in this story may be found. Many able authors have shown the so-called Sacred Scriptures to be unhistorical and pronounced them largely legendary, spurious, and fraudulent.

Beyond the arrangement of this work, little is claimed as original. Ideas, phrases, and even whole paragraphs have been taken from the writings of others and, in most cases, acknowledged.

The most amazing feature of the whole matter is the fraudulent manner in which the Pious Church Fathers made their Holy Bible and the gullibility of the multitude in swallowing the fraud as the "Word of God." After the founding of the Church, an army of trusted, prejudiced scribes went to work under the watchful eye of the Church. A huge task lay ahead. Thousands of scrolls in the great Alexandrian Library had to be examined and some selected for use in making the Bible, while others would be used to compile a revised history of the ancient world.

For the Church would naturally make ancient history agree with its claims that the ancient Pagans were a superstitious, heathenish people and the Church was born to lead humanity from the darkness of ignorance into the Light of Knowledge. This nefarious work of the Church Fathers in compiling the Bible and revising ancient history is admitted even by such a Christian authority as the Catholic Encyclopedia.

In Vol. 4, p. 498, appears the statement that it was the customs of the (Christian) scribes to lengthen out here and there, to harmonize passages, or to add their own explanatory material.

It also maintains that "it is the public character of all (Christian) divines to mold and bend the sacred oracles till they comply with their own fancy, spreading them...like a curtain, closing together or drawing them back as they pleased." In Vol. 7, p. 645, it is stated that: "Even the genuine Epistles were greatly interpolated to lend weight to the personal views of their authors." And what could be more informing and enlightening as to the crooked work of the Church Fathers than this statement in Vol. 12, p. 768; "There was need for a revision (of the ancient writings), which is not yet complete, ranging over all that has been handed down from the Middle Ages."

Of this "revision" of ancient history, Sir Godfrey Higgins stated that: "Every ancient author, without exception, has come down to us through the medium of Christian editors who have...corrupted them all" (The Anacalypsis).

In his *Decline and Fall of Rome,* Gibbon asserted that Eusebius, "the greatest of the Christian historians, indirectly confesses that he had related whatever might rebound to the glory of religion and suppressed all that could tend to the disgrace of it."

Dark Ages of Christianity

G. R. S. Mead, in his *"Fragments Of A Faith Forgotten,"* wrote:

The student of Christianity "is amazed at the general ignorance of everything connected with its history and origin. He gradually works his way to a point whence he can obtain an unimpeded view of the remains of the first two centuries (A.D.) and gaze around on the world that he has never heard of at school and of which no word is ever breathed from the pulpit." (p. 11)

The Church claims the gospel Jesus established its religion, and, according to the Bible, he lived in the first century A.D. But there is not a trace of Jesus or Christianity in the first two centuries, and so, historians have termed that period the Dark Ages of Christianity.

No trace of Jesus or Christianity appeared in any period and not earlier than the 4th century, until Christian scribes revised ancient history, as admitted in the Catholic Encyclopedia. For, as we have stated, the Bible and Christianity were unknown until the Church was born.

We do not see in the true history of the first two centuries, as we expect, that world described in the New Testament gospels, nor that Jesus with crowds following him.

Instead, we see a remarkable man named Apollonius, the great Philosopher of the first century, called Pol by his followers and Paul in the Bible, and whose story is told by Prof. Hotema in his work titled Mystery Man Of The Bible, a startling work that amazes its readers and concerning which A. D. Barber, of the Barber Scientific Foundation, Washington, D.C., wrote the publisher as follows:

"A reader fan of mine sent me *"The Mystery Man of The Bible.* "For over forty years my beliefs have been along the lines of this work, which I regard as the greatest literary masterpiece of all time. Anyone who has studied the Bible is certainly missing the most important part of his education if he fails to read this work, and I recommend it most highly to my friends and foes alike. Every man, woman, and child should read it."

We hear Pol shout to his congregation, "Behold, I show you a mystery: We shall not sleep (in death), but we shall ALL be changed" (to Immortality) (1 Corinthians 15:51).

Not just some of us; not just those "that believeth and are baptized," as the Bible says (Mark 16:16), but ALL of us; and ALL means ALL. And this distinguished disciple of Pythagoras describes the Deity of the ancient world not the anthropomorphic God of the Church, but the Astral God of Paganism. Not the Unknown God of the Greeks (Acts 17:23), but the Eternal Solar Essence of the Universe, in which we actually live and move and have our being (Acts 17:28), as explained by Hotema in *"The Soul's Secret."*

Papacy and Forgery

In his book, *Evolution of the Papacy,* F. A. Ridley wrote:

"By the beginning of the 4th Century, the era of religious conflict which ended in the Triumph of Christianity, the Bishops of Rome had 'arrived.' It required only a further development of the contemporary history for the Papacy, the Universal Bishopric, to make its appearance.

"The third century marked the end of Classical Rationalism and the fourth, the Beginning of Medieval Superstition. For the 4th Century...witnessed the definite triumph of Christianity and, concurrently, introduced persecution as a Permanent feature into the European life of the next 1200 years."

With the establishment of the Church, the Age of Papal Forgeries began. The Popes lied, used trickery, and resorted to forged canons to impose their will upon the people. At this point we turn to that great work of Wm. McCarthy, titled *"Bible, Church and God,"* and excerpt the following:

Out of the thousands (of forgeries) came the "Acts of St. Silvester." This base forgery appeared about 430 A.D., and its object was to add more strength to the Pope's temporal powers.

It related a vivid and sensational account of the conversion and baptism of Constantine, telling how, when about to leave for Constantinople (his new capitol), he gave the secular powers over all Europe to the Church and donated to the Roman See — "The City of Rome and all the providences, districts, and cities of Italy, or the Western Regions."

It was one of the most monstrous forgeries of all ages, and the Popes knew it. They knew it was a lie and a fraud intended to deceive; yet they used it for a thousand years to further their corrupt schemes.

After the Church had so successfully gotten away with this forgery for four hundred years, the Popes used the forgery as the foundation of another forgery even more vicious, the "Pseudo Isidorian Decretals."

The forger took Church and other decrees, dated between the fourth and eighth centuries, including the one just described, and built around them a series of laws that made the Church the absolute master of all Europe. In an age of ignorance and credulity, these forgeries readily passed as genuine. The Popes knew they were false, knew they were intended to defraud and deceive, yet for six hundred years they used them — declared them to be genuine, fooling kings and emperors, and, worse yet, denied they were spurious when so proven.

All Popes, from the 4th to the 16th century, took advantage of forgery. ... For more than a thousand years, these and other Church forgeries flourished. The people believed anything and everything the Church reported. Surely, it was the Age of Forgeries, Ignorance, and Deception.

By the beginning of the 6th century, greed and corruption had thrown the Church into chaos. In fifteen years there were six different Popes. Some departed via the murder route. Rome's political ruler, Theodoric the Ostrogoth, sought to break the strangle-hold of the Church by making his servant, Vigilius, Pope.

Then Rome arrayed itself into Roman and Gothic camps. Pope John was imprisoned. The Church conspired against Theodoric, but could not weaken him. Seeing their cause slipping, Pope Silverius, who purchased his office from Theodotus, decided to win by destroying the liberty of Italy. So, he conspired with Justinian the Byzantine Emperor, who sent an army against Rome, and the treacherous Silverius opened the city's gates. Silverius thought himself secure and settled to enjoy Church Luxury. But a woman soon unhorsed him.

It was at this stage of Church Chicanery and Debauchery that one of the most remarkable women of all times appeared — Theodora, wife of Justinian. She was the most notorious prostitute recorded in history. She took a strong dislike for Pope

Silverius and a stronger liking for his enemy, Vigilius, the friend of Theodoric. She wrote to her husband's general, Belisarius, at Rome:

"Trump up a charge against Silverius (the Pope), and send him here." The Pope was quickly charged with treason. That was sufficient — Vigilius was made God's supreme agent in 537 (see Gibbon's *Decline and Fall of Rome*).

This short synopsis we have given of the history of the Popes to this period is but a mild introduction to the historic depravity and immorality to which the Vicars of God sank during the next thousand years,

While all Priests and Popes did not lie and practice chicanery for the "Glory of God," the most of them did. All were not sexual degenerates, but those who were not were few indeed.

The depravity of the Church and its Priests was described by St. Jerome in the lath century; by Priest Salvianus in the 5th, by Bishop Gregory of Tours in the 6th, and by other Church Dignitaries up to and including Martin Luther in the 16th century. And the text, as here given, is largely based upon their reports, (*Bible, Church & God,* pp. 100-102).

The Sun God

The origin of the Jews is more chimerical than that of Jesus. He was "born" in a council of bishops, but the Jews descend from Astral Gods. The biblical history of the Jews begins with Abraham. He is the son of Terah, a Chaldean living in the city of "Ur of the Chaldees" (Genesis 11:26-28).

How did a Chaldean become the ancestor of the "Children of Israel"? By the clever manipulation of the priest and scribe, Ezra. About 100 B.C., a people called Hebiri are first mentioned on the Egyptian monuments as molesting Palestine. Scholars assert that here is the first appearance of the Hebrews as such on the scene of history. There is no prior record of them. The first reference to Jews in the Bible appears in 2 Kings 16:6. The biblical narrative of Abraham, Isaac, and Jacob is fiction, fabricated by Ezra, as shown by Professor Hotema in the *Ancient Sun God*, from which we shall excerpt the following:

The biblical scribe covered the account of the Creation down to the Flood of Noah in the first eleven chapters of Genesis, hurrying thru chapters 10 and 11 as tho in a rush to dispose of that "light" stuff and begin to describe more weighty events. In chapter 12 a different order appears. The first two verses state:

"Now the Lord said to Ab-Ram, Get thee out of thy country and from thy kindred, and from thy father's house and unto a land that I will show thee, and I will make thee a great nation."

Fourteen chapters are then devoted to Ab-Ram, his family, and his work. And his name is changed: "Neither shall thy name any more be called Ab-Ram, but thy name shall be called Abraham; for a Father of many nations have I made thee" (Genesis 17:5). That statement seems quite innocent upon its face, but critics might want an interpretation of the assertion, "For a Father of many nations I have made thee."

As we shall see, that is another one of those tricky half-truths. The Bible is filled with them, for which reason the layman gets no sense out of them. Ur was the seat of the Sun God Ab-Ram, Ab meaning Father and Ram, the head sign of the Zodiac (Aries), meaning Most High. Bara meant Creator of people, Am meaning people (Dunlap p. 75). The Moon God of Ur and the wife of Ab-Ram was Sahra. And so, the Bible says: "The name of Ab-Ram's wife was Sarai" (Genesis 11:29). Quite simple when the facts are known.

During his long captivity in Babylon, Ezra had much time to study Chaldean tradition. He discovered the legend that great races and great men descend from Astral Gods. So, the Jews shall have the same.

Then Ezra slyly conceals the facts with a change of names. That of Ab-Ram is changed to Abraham, and the name of Sarai is changed to Sarah (Genesis 17:5, 15). These tricky changes appear very innocent upon their face; but when we know the facts we discover the fraud.

To make the trick complete, the astral origin of the Jews must begin with the 12th chapter of Genesis, to have the count harmonize with the Twelve Constellations of the Chaldean Zodiac.

And Ezra knew what he meant when he wrote: "A Father of Nations have I made thee." The Chaldeans regarded the Sun as the Generative Principle; and the Bible reveals this in the statement *"Our God (the Sun) is a Consuming Fire"* (Hebrews 12:29).

Then Ezra weaves a fable around these Astral Gods, making them appear as persons. They have children, and some of them go into Egypt, where they "increased abundantly, and multiplied, and waxed exceedingly mighty; and the Land was filled with them" — in a few generations (Exodus 1:7).

The Egyptian records, carved in stone, mention no migration of the "Children of Israel" into that land. The story is a fabler,

Zodiac and Christianity

We follow Astrology as we proceed. The Twelve Tribes of Israel are Zodiacal in Character. The Twelve Fathers of the Hebrews were Astrological Characters. A reading of the 49th chapter of Genesis removes all doubt on that score.

The Zodiac is the Wheels of Ezekiel (1:15) and is symbolized in the word Jacob, which signifies an arch, vault, dome, which is the Zodiac in which is symbolized the ancient story of the Macrocosm and the Microcosm, as Professor Hotema explained in *Ancient Sun God* and the *Flame Divine*. (Contact: www.frontlinebookpublishing.com)

Jacob had twelve sons, and they signify the Twelve Signs of the Zodiac as follows:

1	Reuben, Aquarius	7	Gad, Scorpio
2	Simeon, Pisces	8	Asher, Virgo
3	Levi, Gemini	9	Issachar, Taurus
4	Judah, Leo	10	Zebulun, Cancer
5	Dan, Libra	11	Joseph, Sagitarius
6	Naphtali, Capricorn	12	Benjamin, Aries

"All these are the Twelve Tribes of Israel," says the Bible (Genesis 49:28).

Not only do Ab-Ram, Isaac, and Jacob live and move then and have their being in the Astral World, but so does the gospel Jesus — a fact which accounts for the reason why the Church so bitterly condemned astrology and everything related to that ancient science.

The gospel Jesus was an actor and played many parts in the New Testament. Many plays were written and presented in the centuries preceding the days of Jesus, and some were religious mystery plays. In them, the stage was set, the actors made their appearance, spoke their lines, and made their exits just as they do in the theater today. There is a noteworthy suggestion of the mystery play in the N.T. None of the books of the N.T. presents a biography of Christ, nor do all the books combined. For he had none. In all of them the stage is set, the Christ appears, speaks his lines, and makes his exit to re-appear in a later scene.

At one time he is made to say, "In my Father's house are many mansions" (John 14:2). This refers to the Twelve Houses of the Zodiac. Then Jesus is made to say, "I will come again (John 4:3). And the Christians are still expecting him. That statement is true and correct when properly understood.

The Answer appears in Ancient Astrology. Jesus, the Actor who plays many roles in the Bible, represents in one of them Aries, Head Sign of the Zodiac. During each Grand Cycle of 25,920 years, the Earth passes thru all Twalve Houses of the Zodiac just as the Sun goes thru them in 365.26 days, called a Sidereal Year.

So, the event predicated by the Ancient Astrologers as the Birth of the Sun, not Son, is an important one that occurs in a new Zodiacal Sign every 2160 years. This cosmic movement causes Aries, Ram, Lamb of God (John 1:29), to return every 25,920 years and each time to reign for 2160 years.

That is the golden secret of the return of Jesus that caused the Church to condemn Astrology so vehemently and to destroy all the ancient astrological records. The 49th chapter of Genesis is more   astrological fable. The Twelve Tribes of Israel symbolize the Twelve Signs of the Zodiac.

Gerald Massey insists that "Israel in Egypt" was not an ethnical entity, but the astrological "Children of Ra," the Egyptian Sun God in the "lower Egypt of Amenta, which is entirely mythical" (Kuhn, p. 107).

Herodotus, the ancient historian, makes no mention of either the Israelites or Solomon.

Biblical Terminology

When the Roman Catholic Church was founded in 325 A.D., Eusebius, Bishop of Caesarea, began gathering literature for the Bible. He was chief speaker at the Nicean Council, the leader of Constantine's scheme and did more than anyone else to put it over.

The task of making the Bible was so great that the work was just well started when Eusebius died in 349 A.D. Then, Jerome, a young, fanatical Christian, took over the job; and about 405 A.D., after some eighty years from the time the work began, the first Christian Bible was finished. It was called the Vulgate because its language was so common.

That Bible was far different from the present Bible. The Catholic Encyclopedia (XII, p. 769) admits that under Popes Sixtus V and Clement VIII the Vulgate, AFTER YEARS OF REVISION, attained its present shape. For a thousand years before printing was invented, priests and monks toiled incessantly on the Bible, weighing every word and selecting such as would best serve the scheme of the Church.

To illustrate the tricky use of words in the Bible, we shall cite a passage in Revelation which scholars have run down and discovered what appears from the facts as the original wording. This last book of the Bible was copied from an ancient Hindu scroll, written thousands of years before the world ever heard of the gospel Jesus, and dealt, in dramatic form, with the initiation of the Neophyte in the Ancient Mysteries.

The Apocalyptic drama is couched in terms of Cosmic Phenomena. Its hero is the Sun, its heroine the Moon, and all its other characters are Planets, Stars, and Constellations, while its stage-setting comprises the Sky, Earth, Rivers, and Sea. It elucidates its subject with the glare of lightning, proclaims it with the roar of thunder, emphasizes it with the shock of the earthquake, and reiterates it with the Ocean's voice — the ceaseless murmur of "many waters." Ever it maintains this cosmic terminology, this vast phrasing of Cosmic Phenomena. It is one of the most stupendous allegories ever written.

The esoteric purpose of initiation was to teach the Neophyte how to develop the Power of Seership. That involves the force termed in Yoga literature the Serpentine of Kundalini Power. This force, we are told, activates the Pituitary and Pineal glands in the brain, the organs of the 6th and 7th senses, and produces the prodigious powers of clairaudience and clairvoyance. Now, according to the undisputed meaning of the original Greek text, a certain passage in Revelation should read:

"The EVIDENCE OF RESURRECTION is the POWER OF SEERSHIP."

In the authorized version that passage reads:

"The TESTIMONY OF JESUS is the SPIRIT OF PROPHECY" (Revelations 19:10).

That is one example of thousands in the Bible, showing how the biblical makers distorted then falsified the ancient scriptures, to support the interest of the Church and deceive the masses. No wonder the original scrolls never afterwards saw the light of day. Some of this data we have excerpted from Professor Hotema's work titled *Son Of Perfection*.

(To obtain a copy of *Son of Perfection* — contact: www.frontlinebookpublishing.com).

Chapter 15
The Word of God

"The third century marked the end of classical rationalism, and the fourth marked the beginning of medieval (churchanity) superstition," wrote F. A. Ridley, in *Evolution of the Papacy*.

That was the end in Europe, Asia Minor, and Egypt of the Arcane Science of the Ancient Masters, handed down from the mists of antiquity. From there on, learning and knowledge vanished in the great Roman Empire, and the masses sank into squalor and ignorance, with the advent of the Dark Ages appearing, and the Glorious Sun of Science was not to rise again for more than a thousand years.

During these long centuries of Church Rule, of darkness and nightmare, of horror and persecution, of faggot and blood, humanity stumbled blindly on, and the Mother Church, with the Holy Bible in one hand and Bloody Sword in the other, forced man to believe that he is lower than the most despicable worm.

By trickery, fraud, falsehood, persecution, and slaughter, the "Word of God" was forced upon the masses; and the Mother Church enveloped the multitude in a psychic atmosphere that constrained man to believe that he is hopelessly lost in the thraldom of sin and headed for the most horrific perdition and punishment possible to imagine, unless he meekly acknowledges all this to be true and cringingly clings to the gown of the mythical Savior, presented by the Mother Church as the only begotten Son of God in the sky, that whosoever believeth in him should not perish, but have everlasting life (John 3:16).

Who can believe Life is not subject to law? Who can believe that Life is ruled by what man believes? It required an age of darkness and an ignorant multitude for the Mother Church to grow rich and powerful on that gigantic fraud. How did it happen that the world came to have a book called the Holy Bible? Why was it compiled from Jewish writings? These are more dark secrets which the Mother Church has tried hard to hide from the light of day. There was no Holy Bible when Constantine founded the Roman State Church in the 4th century. Until then no Bible had been needed. The ancient religious systems had their scriptures and used them. But a new system had now been born, and new literature was needed The ancient scriptures had to be revised to make them promote this new system and to give it suitable standing with the people. So, a Holy Bible, the solemn Word of God, became a vital necessity.

The newly established Mother Church must be based upon and supported by the highest authority that the human mind could conceive; and that authority must emanate from the highest source that the human mind could invent. That was the pressing exigency that produced the Church God in the sky and His Bible, containing His commandments and decrees. It was a clever trick of crafty men, and it made the Mother Church the richest and strongest institution on earth.

God in the Sky

We now come to the secret as to why the Jewish scrolls were selected for the making of the Holy Bible.

The Jews were found to be the only ancient race that believed in a God in the sky, and the Mother Church brags about it. This belief grew out of their seventy years of Babylonian captivity. All those gloomy years they had prayed for some power to liberate them from bondage.

Then came Cyrus, the Persian king. He conquered Babylonia, liberated the Jews, and sent them back to

Jerusalem. Now they were certain their prayers had been heard and answered by a God in the sky.

The Church Fathers were so delighted over this discovery that they overplayed the God Game in making their Holy Bible. They were so confused about Gods that they included several, like shooting in the dark and hoping to hit the target by accident and ring the bell.

One of these Gods had a long discussion with a man called Moses, and he showed Moses his back parts. Whether from the waist up or down, the Holy Bible fails to say (Exodus 33:21-23). Another God was just a Spirit which no man had ever seen at any time (John 4:24; 1 John 4:12). Still another God was a Consuming Fire (Hebrews 12:29).

The other ancient nations had no God in the sky. Their gods were their conceptions that represented the powers and processes of the Universe as presented in Nature — the deified patrons of husbandry and science. Such gods were useless to the Mother Church. Science has nothing the Mother Church wanted, and husbandry was for slaves.

The Great Library

Ptolemy Philadelphus (309-2116 B. C.), a learned Egyptian scholar of his day, offered rich rewards for scientific scrolls and philosophic manuscripts for his great library at Alexandria. Impelled by their desire for the reward, wise men of all nations went to Egypt with their choicest writings; and by this means, Philadelphus succeeded in securing some 250,000 of the greatest scriptures in the world.

And so, to this library went the Church Biblical Committee to examine the scrolls and to select such as were the most suitable for the Mother Church.

A careful search disclosed the fact that the Jewish writings were the best for the Mother Church. It was these writings only that sung high praises to a God in the sky, the God whom the Jews imagined had heard and answered their prayers in the past for help. According to their own history, apparently written by them, the Jews were a small, weak, luckless race that suffered much at the hands of neighboring nations.

In the second book of the Holy Bible, the Jews appear as slaves in Egypt (Exodus 1:13), and a mythical character called Moses, unknown outside of the Bible, had an urgent conference with the Jewish God who directed Moses to go and make life miserable for Pharaoh until he liberated the enslaved Jews.

The job was well done, and the Jews were liberated and led by Moses to freedom, says the story.

Then later they suffered another siege of bondage, being taken into Babylonian captivity for seventy years.

This time they had no Moses to help them. So, they prayed loud and long to a super-natural power for aid. And they were certain their prayers were heard and answered when Cyrus conquered Babylonia and sent them back to Palestine. And so, Cyrus was hailed by the Jews "as a divinely appointed savior, the anointed one of their J H V H , the God of the sky."

God's Chosen People

The evidence discovered by archeologists in the last two centuries shows that "God's Chosen People" consisted of a small band of illiterate sheep herders, and the Pious Church Fathers made their Holy Bible build this little, unlearned group up to where it was one of the great races of antiquity.

The Word of God says: "Ye shall be a peculiar treasure unto me above all people. ... For thou art a holy people unto the Lord thy God; and the Lord thy God hath chosen thee to be a special people unto him, above all people that are upon the face of the earth" (Exodus 19:5; Deuteronomy 7:6).

That was a deliberate forgery, intended to trick, dupe, and deceive the world; and it required an age of darkness and ignorance to make people believe that glaring falsehood.

The feebleness of these "holy people" appears in the statement that Nebuchadnezzar (604-561 B.C.), in three raids sent there, found only 4600 people which he saw fit to carry away. And these 4600 Jews formed the famous "Captivity" (Jeremiah 52:27-30). Also, the Mother Church claims these people were never polytheists but always Monotheists, and worshipped only one God — Jehovah. The Bible itself proves that this claim is more fraud added to fraud.

The worship of Jahveh or Yahveh, the God of the desert whom the Israelites had brought with them, was quite compatible with the simultaneous worship of Astarte, the Goddess of Fertility, and of numerous other local gods, bulls, sacred trees, and family fetishes such as were venerated in ancient society generally.

Yahveh was just one God among many, a "Baal" like all the rest, and was worshipped with sacred prostitution and human sacrifices, according to the Bible.

Many instances of this concept of Yahveh appear in the Bible and no telling how much of it the Pious Bible Makers eliminated. He is the rain-god, who brings the flood (Genesis 7). The rainbow is a token of his promise not to do it again (Genesis 9). He blessed the fields (Genesis 27:27); is appeased by human sacrifice (Judges 11:30-4; 2 Samuels 21). He sends fire from heaven to destroy his enemies (Genesis 19; 2 Kings 1), or to consume a sacrifice that particularly pleased him (1 Kings 18; 1 Chronicles 21:26; 2 Chronicles 7:1).

"God's Chosen People" worshipped a Bull, Apis, and the sun, moon, stars, and all the host of heaven. They worshipped fire and kept it burning on an altar. They worshipped stones, an oak tree, and bowed down to images. They worshipped a Queen of Heaven called Astarte or Mylitta and burnt incense to her. They worshipped Baal, Moloch, and. Chemosh and offered up human sacrifices to them after which, in some cases, they ate the victim (Psalms 106:28, 37, 38; Ezekiel 16:20).

And the Word of God states that his "Chosen People" were polythiests, polygamists, indolaters, and fire worshippers who burned their children as sacrifices, who butchered their foes to the last suckling infant, and who honored traitors, assassins, and prostitutes who served their interest.

According to the Holy Bible, any crime may be committed in the name or for the sake of this God (Ex. 32:26-28; Deuteronomy 13:6-10; etc.).

While in Babylonian captivity, the "Chosen People" were taught to read and write; and they learned the Babylonian legends of the Creation, the Garden of Eden, Eve and the Serpent, Noah and the Flood, etc. These legends they later incorporated in their writings, and they appear in the Holy Bible.

And, quite logically, the Jews included in their writings touching lyrics of unlimited praise of their "God in Heaven," who liberated them twice, as they thought, in answer to their prayers. When the Biblical Committee of the Mother Church found these Jewish writings in the Alexandrian Library, they had just about what they wanted.

And then with prolific distortion, deletion, and interpolation, in which work the Biblical Committee were experts, the Word of God took shape and was skillfully prepared; and then it was proclaimed to the world by the Mother Church as being "Divinely Inspired." To question the claim meant to invite death by burning.

Facts and Fiction

A remarkable feature of the Holy Bible is the skillful manner in which the expert compilers wove facts and fiction together. We defy anyone to read one chapter in the Bible, or one paragraph, and find either truth of falsehood separately stated. And that is the reason why it took so long to make the first draft of the Holy Bible. The work was begun in 325 A.D., and that first draft was not finished until early in the 5th century. For every word, every phrase, every line, every sentence, and every paragraph had to be carefully weighed and considered in order to make everything the more favorable for the Mother Church.

And it is extremely shocking to know that supposedly intelligent and honorable men will deliberately lie, beguile, and falsify in their efforts to make the deceived, mind-controlled masses believe that the Holy Bible is the Divinely Inspired Word of God.

The Bishop of Manchester (England), writing in the Manchester Examiner and Times, said:

"The very foundation of our faith, the very basis of our hopes, the very dearest of our consolations are taken from us when one line of that sacred volume, on which we base everything, is declared to be untruthful and untrustworthy" (Doane, p. 17).

Each falsehood in the Bible is craftily and inseparably connected with an undeniable truth, and yet the true and false are so intricately and delicately interwoven that it is utterly impossible for the unprepared mind to separate the one from the other.

Chained in Darkness

The Holy Bible has gone out to the world and chained in darkness, as intended by the Mother Church, a larger number of people than any other secular book has ever done.

And these tricked, deceived, and duped victims of the Mother Church must live in that darkness until they shall have evolved to such mental ability that they can winnow facts from fiction and truth from falsity and come to understand the falseness.

The Holy Bible is the greatest book of distortion, interpolation, fraud, falsehood, fiction, and mis-representation that man has ever produced, and the purpose of the work was human enslavement.

H. M. Tichenor said: "The Bible binds in slavery the body and brain of man. ... No ruler nor exploiter. ... could outrage the race more than have the Christian exploiting and war-making powers" (*Sun Worship,* p. 15).

No system of human enslavement in all the history of the world has been so clever, cunning, and complete as that termed Roman Catholicism; and that called Protestant Christianity is just one short step better.

The men who made the Bible knew no more than we do about who wrote the scrolls from which they compiled the Bible. And then they destroyed the scrolls to conceal their actual contents from the eyes of the world. The oldest manuscript of the Old Testament extant is dated 916 A.D. The older scrolls and manuscripts have been destroyed or concealed to hide the facts which the biblical makers did not want the world to know. The Bible is presented as being wholly Jewish in origin. But the Jews for centuries were captive and slaves of other nations, and they built the scrolls of the Old Testament upon the legends, traditions, myths, and folklore of these other nations.

For almost four hundred years after the time of the gospel Jesus, there was no Bible. Parts of the Septuagint had been compiled and translated into Latin, but no complete version existed.

During the latter part of the 4th century and the early part of the 5th, a young fanatic named Jerome, using the Septuagint, built around it the Latin Bible, called the Vulgate because its language was so common. Twelve hundred years after that, at the Council of Trent, the Catholic Bishops decreed the Vulgate to be the true "Word of God." The masses do not know that the ancient writings from which the Old Testament was compiled consisted of poetry, fables, fiction, drama, legends, tradition, etc.

There are still five poetical books in the Bible that were not changed to prose — Job, Psalms, Proverbs, Ecclesiastes, and Canticles or Song of Solomon. These un-metrical hymns of poetical character were originally arranged for chanting and are still so used in many churches for the direct purpose of arousing the emotions and unbalancing the mind — a trick not difficult to do when it is known that 90% of the brain cells in the best of us are latent and dormant.

Man's emotions are equivalent to the sum total of his sentient powers. As the aroused emotions unbalance the Mind and control the man, he does things he would not otherwise do. Thus, exoteric religion thrives on blind credulity and disordered imagination.

As poetry, the original scriptures possessed an imaginative quality of thought and a figurative mode of expression This is now used to the limit to arouse the emotions and affect the Mind. In fact, the Mother Church contends that it should control the Mind and that humanity should not think otherwise than as taught by the Church. The original scriptures contained no vowels; and vowels were not introduced until the 7th century.

Then it was that the Four Sacred Letters of the mysterious word J.H.V.H. were first vowelized. That was hundreds of years after the days of Moses and indirectly gives us the approximate time when the biblical makers invented the interpolation in Chapter VI of Exodus, reading:

"And I appeared unto Abraham, unto Isaac, and Unto Jacob, by the name of God Almighty, but by the name Je Ho Vah was I not known to them."

The vowels were borrowed from the Syrians, and punctuation marks were not used until the 15th century. The semi-colon was not used in the Bible until after 1582. It was then that the contents of the Bible were first divided into chapters and verses, the purpose being to make easier of execution the fraud of falsification, interpolation, deletion, and distortion.

The English Bible

Prior to the 14th century there was no English Bible. It began to take shape under John Wyclif (1320- 1384) and his coworkers. They gathered material here and there and translated the Latin Vulgate into an English version in the years 1378-80, deleting, distorting, and interpolating the context to suit their purposes and opinions. Now, for the first time, this work put the Bible within reach of the masses, and they were highly curious to learn at last something about the mysterious "Word of God" in the sky.

After Wyclif's Bible, other versions began to appear so fast and were so discordant and corrupted that England, in alarm, passed a law in 1408 prohibiting the translation of Latin Bible into English. Then, in 1525, appeared Tyndale's Bible, prepared by him after he was driven from England for translating the Bible into English. It was the most loved, and most hated, and the most successful of all.

One half of the Christians bought it to read, and the other half, to burn. Six thousand copies of it were burned in a huge bonfire in London.

The church authorities finally captured Tyndale at Antwerp in 1535. He was tried for heresy and condemned. His only crime was translating the Bible into the English language. On Oct. 6, 1536, he was strangled at the stake and his body burnt. He crowned his work with untimely death, but his efforts were not in vain. At that time the Mother Church declared: "Anyone found guilty of reading the Bible in English must forfeit land, cattle, and goods from his heirs forever."

What the Mother Church has done it will do again when it has the power to do it. For their English Bible, the Roman Catholics adopted the Vulgate, translated other versions into Greek, and then retranslated the Greek back into English. Then on the title page was placed this deceptive notice:

"Translated out of the original Greek and with the former translation diligently compared and revised."

Concerning this, M. M. Mangasarian wrote: "If the translators of the Bible had wished to confine themselves to the facts, instead of saying "Translated out of the original Greek," which is not so, they would have said this on the title-page of their work:

"A Collection of Writings
Of Unknown Date and Authorship
Rendered Into English
From Supposed Copies of Supposed Originals."

The Rev. T. K. Cheyne, one of the contributors to the most scholarly work produced by churchmen (the Encyclopedia Biblica), gives a number of instances of deliberate manipulation of the Bible text by the translators. He said:

"The Old Testament is not altogether in its original form. It has undergone not merely corruption, but also editorial manipulation."

This is the work of man, not of God. No God had anything to do with it. He did nothing and said nothing in any form of writing. And now He is blamed for what men have done.

History tells us that there have been more than 1800 conflicting versions of the Holy Bible, compiled from more than 8000 scrolls and manuscripts. Which one of them is the true "Word of God"?

New Testament

After the various books of the New Testament had been collected and translated from the original tongue into Greek, the first printed edition of the whole of the Greek N.T. was that contained in the Complutensis Polygot, published by Francis Ximenes de Cisneros. The chief editor of the work was Lopez de Stunica. It was printed in Greek and Latin and completed in 1514. That of Erasmus was published in 1516, also in Greek and Latin. Then, in 1535, Erasmus published his 5th edition, which is the basis of the Common Text.

The Greek manuscripts used for these editions were few in number, of little critical value, and hence do not possess much real authority. In 1546 and 1549 Robert Stephens printed two small editions of the Greek New Testament, and in 1550 his folio edition with various readings from several manuscripts. He collected some fifteen manuscripts, all different, but followed chiefly the Complutensian copy.

Griesbach published his first edition in 1775 and his last in 1806. He combined in his work the   results of the collections of others. Since Griesbach, several other editions have been published and received the approval of scholars. The number of manuscripts of the New Testament now known, and which have been examined, is nearly 700, all different. Which one is the correct one?

English Versions

The first English version of the New Testament was made by John Wyclif about 1367, but no part of it was printed before 1731. Tyndalets translation was published at Antwerp of Hamburg in 1535. Coverdale published the whole Bible in English in 1535. He followed his interpreters and adopted Tyndale's version.

The Great Bible was published in 1539. Cranmer's Bible was published in 1540 and was essentially the same as the Great Bible. The Bishops Bible was published in 1568. The Doway Bible appeared it 1609.

The King James: Bible, or so-called Authorized Version that was authorized by no one, was published in 1611, Forty-seven persons were appointed as a committee in 1604 in an effort to put the Bible in shape and kill off the various discordant versions. They were directed to use the Bishops Bible and to alter it as little as the original would allow.

Since 1611 many translations of the Bible have been published. The version in common use was not translated from the original, but is a revision of the versions then in use. What the original scriptures said, no one knows. And the Bible we have presents the opinions and conclusions of those who translated the various manuscripts, and these opinions and conclusions are in harmony with the views of the Mother Church.

The Ancient Scriptures

To ascribe the biblical books to any set of authors, as the makers of the Bible have done, is to trespass on the ground of sheer folly and base falsehood. In the common sense of the term, the books of the Bible were never "written" at all. No set of men ever sat down and composed them out of their thoughts, observations, experiences, and knowledge. What the ancient scrolls actually contained were the outlines of ancient tradition and legend, formulated by the accumulated wisdom of ancient sages, covering the observations and experiences of mankind for perhaps a million years.

Out of that wisdom there came forth those set formulations of cosmic data, cosmic laws, and moral codes that have survived the test of time and still stand as scientific commitments. For that accumulated wisdom presents in fable, fiction, parable, allegory, symbol, and dramatic Poetry, the substantial facts of life, collected and correlated by the ancient masters and not yet understood by the clergy, who see in such writings various things that are not there. And furthermore, the work in its entirely is so puzzling and profound that sixteen hundred years of the most consecrated effort of modern scholars to fathom its meaning has left its esoteric message still unrevealed, as Hotema so clearly shows in his *"Son of Perfection."*

The time of increasing knowledge has come when persistent workers and unprejudiced investigators are gradually stripping the deceptive mask of literary disguise from the face of the ancient scriptures.

And it comes as a startling surprise for one to discover that what has been gratuitously assumed to be the produce of primitive naiveté and heathenish superstition is now seen to be the variegated cloak of a recondite wisdom.

Not only do the strange symbols and peculiar allegories bear the impress of genius competent to portray cosmic facts in ridiculous figures and ludicrous fables, but these ancient authors register an equal skill in their artful concealment. The employment by the ancient sages of the crafty disguise has carried them so far beyond us in knowledge and skill that we have been lulled into accepting the disguise for the actual fact. Well, that is, under the pressure of the priesthood, with the bitter alternative of burning for doubting.

By the dawning light of a better day, we begin to see that the authors of the ancient scrolls were master dramatists and expert poets. The scrolls were first prepared as dramatic poetry; and the changing of the Bible from poetry to prose was not completed until the 14th century.

With soft touches and deft strokes did the ancient sages weave their profound pattern of terranic life, of astral powers, and physical phenomena, thru their clever narratives of gods, men, mermaids, harpies, satyrs, centaurs, sphinxes, serpents, stags, dragons, boars, bulls, of labyrinths, mountains, seas, rivers, whirlwinds, clouds of fire and falling stars, that not one of the most outlandish details of their fabrications can be ignored, without the loss of some signal link of meaning.

Generations of scholars, chained for a thousand years by the Mother Church in the cave of theological darkness, have perennially scoffed the suggestion that the ancient myths might be fanciful portrayals of esoteric facts. And these dupes of darkness have charged the Chaldeans, Babylonians, Egyptians, and Greeks, the most enlightened races known in history, with possessing the mentality of immature children.

We have stupidly accused them of taking their three-headed dogs, fire-breathing dragons, beasts with seven heads and ten horns, their griffins, naids, Cyclops, Circuses, and Medusas, for definite actualities.

As to the New Testament, it is a great error to think that it is a simple book for the masses and that it is intelligible to the simple and humble. We quickly change our mind on that point when we peruse *Son of Perfection* by Hotema, in which he shows that the last book of the bible is a scientific treatise dealing with the Living Fire and that the Book With Seven Seals is actually the human body (Revelation 5).

A mere literary analysis of the style of the content of the Four Gospels indicates the immense power of these narratives, cleverly presented in symbols and allegories. They are composed of fables, fiction and drama, and were written consciously for a definite purpose, by experts and scientists who knew much more than they wrote, and who concealed in allegory what they said.

The Gospels relate in a direct and definite manner to the existence of esoteric teachings, and they are in themselves one of the chief literary evidences of the existence of esotericism.

Nor is there any evidence for believing that the Gospels were written by the persons to whom they are indirectly ascribed, i.e., the immediate disciples of the gospel Jesus. For there was no such person, and nowhere in all history can there be found a set of men answering to the description of the twelve disciples. They are utterly unknown outside of the New Testament.

It is a much more logical supposition that the Four Gospels had a very long and different history, and their substance was written ages before. The oldest known texts, i.e., the Greek and first Latin translations, are much more abstract than are the later translations. There is much in the earlier text that appears in the form of an abstract idea, which, in the later translations, has developed into a concrete figure.

Occult students know that Revelation, last book of the N.T., was written by Hindu Masters thousands of years before the world ever heard of the gospel Jesus, as Hotema shows in *Son of*

Perfection; and this means that every reference to Jesus in Revelation is a spurious interpolation, knowingly made by the pious biblical makers, and especially designed to bring into the picture their fraudulent Jesus, the only begotten Son of their God. Nor is Revelation a work of prophesy as the Mother Church teaches. It does not predict future events. The Ancient Masters were not engaged in that sort of superstition and deception. They were interested in Man and his improvement, which the Mother Church is not, and to that end they directed their studies and shaped their patterns.

Revelation deals strictly and entirely with Man and His Body but in particular it treats of the Living Fire of the Universe and its action within the living organism.

One will understand this better after reading *The Flame Divine* by Hotema, in which he reveals the great secret of Life. He shows that the Living Fire, as Cosmic Electricity, penetrates the Brain at the Fonticulus Frontalis in the crown of man's head and flows down the Spinal Cord for super-refining in the Creative Centers at the base of the Spinal Column. And then if the Living Fire is not consumed on the low level of animalistic propagation, it flows back to the Brain, activating, in its ascension, the Six Great Nerve Centers of the Body, and, upon entering the Brain, it resurrects the latent powers of the Pituitary and Pineal glands, allegorically described in the Bible as "the marriage of the Lamb" (Revelation 19:7).

And the startling result of this resurrection is the Birth of the Godly Man, who is symbolized in the Bible as the Blazing Star of Bethlehem (Mar. 2:2) and who stands so high above the common level of Consciousness that he is termed a SEER, possessing the rare powers of Premonition and Clairvoyance, as ascribed to the gospel Jesus (John 1:47), all of which Hotema covers in detail in *Son of Perfection*.

The great physician and scientist, Dr. George W. Crile, discovered the Living Fire, and published a paper in 1932 in which he stated that in every atom in the human body there is a Solar Center, having a temperature approximately equal to that of the Sun's surface. That is the secret of Life.

The presence of the Living Fire in the Body was known to the Ancient Masters, and they discovered that it can be intensified and how to do it, with the amazing result that such men are exalted to the rare state of Consciousness where they were called the Sons of God (Genesis 6:2) and also Masters (John 3:10), They were of that exalted class which was said to be as free of Carnal Lust as the Angels of Heaven (Mark 12:25).

Now we can understand why Paul opposed marriage and favored it only as the lesser of two evils (1 Corinthians 7:9). Then, as we take another look in the Bible, we observe, as might well be expected, that some of this exalted class weakened mentally and became "back-sliders." For they unwisely looked and they "saw the (beautiful) daughters of men (who were not Initiates of the Light) that they were fair; and they took them wives of all which they chose" (Genesis 6:2) and engaged in the work of producing families instead of philosophy. This particular phase of the Ageless Wisdom is covered by the symbolism of Card No. 6 of the Ancient Tarot, titled "Temptation," and in the Bible it appears in chapters 2 and 3 of Genesis, in which is allegorically taught one of the greatest lessons of life yet ignored by the Clergy because the profound nature of the teachings is not understood by them.

Ancient Myths

When the Ancient Masters invented fiction and fable to explain some cosmic phenomena, they may not have intended to start a religious belief or theory. But the crafty priesthood, ever alert, grasped these opportunities for use in spreading the scope of their power.

The fable of Adam and Eve, for instance, has traveled practically around the world, carried by the priesthood. It was known in most of Asia and Africa when Europe was practically terra incognita. Later, it was disseminated thruout Europe and, upon the discovery of the Western World, it was carried there also by the priesthood. In Ceylon, at Adam's Peak, there is a footprint said to have been made by Adam, to which stupid pilgrimages were made many centuries ago by the early inhabitants of that Island when our European ancestors were living in cages. This alleged footprint of Adam is probably just as authentic as the one of Jesus, which is shown to the suckers in the garden convent on the Mount of Olives, near Jerusalem.

The names Adam and Eve originated in India not in Palestine. They are Sanskrit, not Jewish, and the early Jews probably got their account of Genesis from East Indian sources, just as they got the Hindu scroll which became Revelation.

As previously stated, the myth is known to many races, but in some cases with different names and modified details. It was accepted into the sacred scriptures of the Hindus, Jews, Christians, Mohammedans, etc., and is believed in by millions of people who regard it as a fact and not a fable.

About the time of the beginning of our Era, there seems to have been a period of unrest among the thinkers of the world, as there is today Greek philosophy, Platonism, Neo-Platonism, Manichaeism, Montanism, Gnosticism, made great inroads on the older faiths, and Judaism underwent many changes.

Then appeared Christianity, guided by crafty men who left these other systems, taking with them all the other competing ideas and adopting a policy of making converts by adapting itself to their views, so as not to make a change from one of the other faiths to Christianity too abrupt or difficult.

That policy worked so well that when the Mother Church was organized, it took over everything that it could and then invented Christian explanations for the Pagan Festivals, philosophy, etc.

In this way the faith of the early Christians became swamped with foreign ideas, but the Church Fathers skillfully ironed out the wrinkles and amalgamated all the frills into one more or less congruous mass of doctrines. And so, it has been well said that "Modern Christianity is founded on pre-Christian Paganism and post-Christian metaphysics."

The Gods

"We are led by Nature to think there are gods, and we discover by reason of what nature they are" (Cicero).

In regard to Gods, Dr. James Clark has this to say: "Of all the Life Games which have bemused, confused, and bedeviled Man, none has contributed more to the tragic situation in his affairs than the 'God Game.' But for the fact that Man has been operating entirely on a functional basis or belief and deductive thought, these long, bloody centuries of "Civilization" and "Culture" need never have occurred" (Eternal Time).

Some authorities explain the myths of the gods as a deification of cosmic forces and phenomena. Thus, rivers are the Sons of Terra (earth) and Oceanus (ocean). The evaporated water from the Ocean falls on the Earth, forming streams and rivers. The story of the War of the Gods and Titans becomes merely an allegorical account of the Conduct of the Elements, as the howl of the hurricane, the glare of lightning, the roar of thunder. Some ancient philosophers saw in these fables only a physical, ethical, or historical explanation of the Universe. But the crafty priesthood presented them differently to the masses.

Eumerides said there is nothing supernatural and that mythologists were merely attempting a historical explanation of physical facts. The early Christians, like Augustine, rather favored this view, and they thought that Zeus, Aphrodite, and the other Gods and Goddesses were originally real persons, not divine but diabolical, who had become transformed by tradition into deities.

Porphyry ascribed to the myths of the gods a meaning which was partly moral and partly theosophical. The religious elements were for the purpose of supporting the law and controlling the masses.

This was also the opinion of Aristotle, who considered the stories as allegories, invented by statesmen and legislators "to persuade the many and to support the law," Plutarch, in an essay on Superstition, said that "Ignorance about the gods which makes the obstinate man an atheist, also begets credulity in weak and pliant minds," The atheist fears nothing because he believes there is nothing to fear. The ignorant and superstitious believe in gods and fear them because they are thought to be unfriendly.

Dr, James Clark says: "There has been no example in the whole of history's legends to compare with the record of (the biblical) 'God' as a cruel and ruthless mass killer. A shocking example in punitive and corrective procedure to offer mankind, allegedly His own creation, and an example which has been so faithfully and repeatedly emulated right up to the present time, when Man has at last conceived the means whereby he may duplicate it — universal cremation! Truly, 'God is Love.' What a story! What a legend! (Eternal Time)."

He who believes in gods and fears them is never free of fear, whatever may befall him. He extends his fear beyond the grave and believes in the "gates of hell" (Matthew 16:18) and its fires, in the darkness, the ghosts, the infernal judges, etc. And the Mother Church and the standardized systems by which civilization is ruled are determined to keep the masses in fear and darkness and to discredit and persecute the few who get their eyes open and would spread the Light of Knowledge.

THE END

1960 The Ageless Wisdom of the Ancient Masters teaches us that the Divine Trinity is reflected in man; and this knowledge, when correctly and clearly interpreted as Hotema has presented it in his various works, will lift the veil that darkens the Mind and reveal to the understanding of man the facts of Eternal Life.

www.ingramcontent.com/pod-product-compliance
Lightning Source LLC
Chambersburg PA
CBHW072013290326
41934CB00007BA/1082